THE LAST OF YOUR SPRINGS

THE LAST OF YOUR SPRINGS

Donald Kennedy

Stanford Historical Society
Stanford, California
1998

Stanford Historical Society
Stanford, California
© 1998 by the Stanford Historical Society

Printed in the United States of America

Library of Congress Cataloging-in-Publication Data

Kennedy, Donald, 1931-
    The last of your springs / Donald Kennedy.
        p.   cm.
    Includes index.
    ISBN 0-9664249-0-5 (hc.)
    1. Stanford University--History--20th century.
    2. Baccalaureate addresses.   3. Kennedy, Donald,
1931- .   I. Title.
LD3041.K46   1998
378.794'73--dc21   98-24256
                                                    CIP

To three inspiring predecessors:

David Starr Jordan,
J. E. Wallace Sterling,
and Richard W. Lyman

Acknowledgments

It would be impossible to name all those who made Stanford
University the extraordinary place it has been for me and for so
many others. I have now been a member of its faculty, and thus
of the Stanford family, for 38 years—more than a third of the
University's existence. Over that time faculty colleagues, graduate students, undergraduate advisees, and members of the remarkable Stanford staff have all been important parts of my life.

But in the period 1979–1992, when I served as Provost and
then, for twelve years, as President, a few colleagues have made
a special contribution both to my work and to the events that
form the core of this anthology. Al Hastorf, Jerry Lieberman,
and Jim Rosse were splendid partners-in-arms as Provosts. Bob
Rosenzweig, Bob Freelen, John Ford, and John Schwartz were
important senior colleagues in different roles during especially
challenging times. I will always remember the help I got from
Marlene Wine, Phyl Stevens, Bob Hamrdla, and Joan Parker.
Ted Mitchell was an invaluable source of strength and support
during the transition at the end of my presidency. And for his
wise and thoughtful counsel on student matters, as well as for
instruction in the "teachable moment," I thank Jim Lyons. Many
other people, some of them mentioned in the course of this ac-

count of events, were important as well, and I regret that I cannot tell them all of my gratitude.

Throughout my time at Stanford, I have been privileged to serve with a hugely talented, diverse faculty. I want especially to thank my colleagues, present and past, in the Department of Biological Sciences, for their support and their continuing willingness to recognize me as a colleague even after I had strayed. My newer associates in the Institute for International Studies have supplied me amply with the joys of reconstituted scholarly life, while remaining patient with my slow reacclimatization. And during difficult times, colleagues from everywhere reminded me, time after time, of their commitment to the institution and to their students.

The Stanford student body has delighted and amazed me for over half my life. Collectively, they provided me with unexpected relief from one discouragement after another—some of which, of course, they had caused in the first place. They also convinced me, again and again, that there is great hope for our future. This book is really about, and for, them.

This project had a long and occasionally troubled history. For this happy ending, I thank the Stanford Historical Society and its officers—Rosemary MacAndrew, Karen Bartholemew, Roxanne Nilan, and (especially) Maggie Kimball. I was exceptionally fortunate to have Janet Gardiner as an editor. She was splendidly skillful, and beyond that supplied an enthusiasm for the project that buoyed my own confidence in it. My old friend Bill Kaufmann, Mr. Flood, lent a world of experience and support, secular as well as spiritual. It couldn't have happened without him.

Finally, it is a joy to thank Robin Kennedy for being a source of solace, inspiration, and the occasional nudge in the interest of this project. She has loved Stanford as I have, and her help, editorial and otherwise, has been indispensable.

Contents

Introduction   1

1. Beginning: 1980–1981   5

2. Speaking Out: 1981–1982   24

3. Early Controversies: 1982–1983   42

4. Looking Outward: 1983–1984   57

5. Divisions: 1984–1985   75

6. Divestment and Obligation: 1985–1986   85

7. Hard Choices: 1986–1987   103

8. Culture Wars: 1987–1988   120

9. Talking About Race: 1988–1989   133

10. Gorbachev Meets Loma Prieta: 1989–1990   162

11. Centennial: 1990–1991   182

12. Saying Goodbye: 1991–1992   204

Index   219

Eight pages of illustrations follow p. 102

THE LAST OF YOUR SPRINGS

Introduction

This book began as a collection of farewell talks, given each Commencement from 1981 to 1992 to the graduates of Stanford University.

The occasion of commencement is a little like a wedding: joyful, celebratory, and often not very memorable. The content of commencement addresses, like the words of officiants at marriage ceremonies, fades quickly. Fortunately, by tradition, the President of Stanford University does not deliver the usual commencement address. An outsider of high distinction, selected by a committee, has that duty. The president delivers a personal farewell to the graduates at the very end of the ceremony.

For me that was always an important occasion, and I prepared harder for it than for any other public appearance during the academic year. Each time the obligation fell to me, I faced a choice. As I saw it then, I could select some important policy issue or societal challenge, and talk about that; or I could comment on some theme or themes that had developed during the academic year, perhaps combining that with some candid advice-giving. The latter seemed more dangerous but also more appropriate. In the early 1980s, it struck me that university faculties and, even more, university presidents were strikingly hesitant to do anything that might cast them in an avuncular, let alone paternal, role. But the delivery of honest adult advice, as long as it springs from authentic caring and has some relevant experience behind it, is a function no teacher should shun. Otherwise the field would be left clear for the professional messengers of virtue—politicians, evangelicals, and the authors of self-help books—leaving everyone asking: "But where are the teachers?"

There was another reason as well, springing from my own personal background and some derived convictions. I was raised in New England, by parents who had been born there (my mother was from Berlin, New Hampshire) or had spent most of a life there (my father, though born in Ohio, was educated at Williams and Harvard, and his career in publishing began in Boston). My mother taught at, and I attended for a time, a rather progressive private elementary school. Part of my boyhood was spent in Deerfield, Massachusetts, where I actually remember the legendary headmaster Frank Boyden—the subject of one of John McPhee's wonderful books—hitting grounders to the Deerfield Academy infield before a game, at the ripe young age of seventy-five. (Later, as a student at yet another independent school, I returned to play soccer at Deerfield.) Many of my parents' friends, as well as two aunts and an uncle, were teachers in New England schools.

Often as President of Stanford I was asked what the job was like. I replied that part of the time one feels like a chief executive officer of a large corporation, and part of the time like a headmaster. Plainly I liked the latter part better; equally plainly, I brought to it some convictions about the school's responsibility for the whole person. It seemed natural to talk to students about their lives, not just about what we were putting into their heads.

So I began in that vein in 1981, and kept the basic format for a dozen years. After I left the presidency in 1992, I was asked occasionally whether I had ever collected the commencement farewells. That led to a tentative plan to gather them for some sort of informal publication. When I looked them over, two things became clear. First, by themselves they made a pretty thin collection. Second, the themes behind them required some elaboration in order to provide a context. Thus I thought of providing other things I had written, mostly during the academic year preceding each farewell, in order to supply the needed background. I have also written introductions to each piece, and added explanatory notes to help the reader—especially the reader not intimately familiar with Stanford lore.

As will be apparent, the exercise has turned into an annualized history of a dozen years in Stanford's life. It was a period of significant growth for the University. Stanford rebuilt its physical base for doing modern science, continued a remarkable record of growth in prestige and attractiveness to students, changed the complexion of the student body, and met the goal of the largest capital fund-raising campaign ever undertaken by a university. But it was also a period of intense challenge. Controversy over South African investments and allegations of lingering racism produced campus rifts in the mid-1980s that were difficult to heal. Proposals for change in the Western Culture curriculum were much exaggerated by those outside the University, provoking charges that Stanford was adopting a form of "cultural relativism." There were a series of policy differences with the federal government, including allegations that Stanford and other universities had conspired to fix tuition and financial aid levels. And in 1991, a Congressional committee held hearings in which Stanford (and later, other universities) were accused of improper indirect cost recovery, questionable expenditures for the President's house, and collusion with government officials. Even the eventual clearing of the University and its officers, and a favorable financial settlement with the sponsoring government agency, did not entirely remove the taint nor fully undo the financial damage caused by this dispute.

The years 1980–1992 were thus difficult, rewarding, exciting years; and each brought stresses and opportunities to the Stanford community that could hardly be ignored in the rite of pas-

sage that ends each year. I tried on each occasion not to ignore
or to soften the difficulties—even if they had engaged me personally. Every life that is fully lived contains moments of challenge, of trauma, and of defeat. To talk of knowing without en-
gaging with the matter of coping, it seems to me, would delete a
vital element of the teacher's duty.

The non-Stanford reader will, despite my efforts to supply
context and explanation, experience certain difficulties. Here on
what is affectionately called The Farm there is a peculiar local
argot; it consists of abbreviating the names of place and things
by combining their first syllables. Thus Memorial Church is
known as MemChu, and frozen yogurt as FroYo. The farewells
to the graduates with which each year ends are laced with these
and other local references. They also begin and end with a ritu-
alized coda. It was tempting to edit these out in order to avoid
repetition. Instead I left them in, because each of the talks was
directed to a particular set of people who are entitled to read it as
it was said to them.

Finally, it will not escape the reader's notice that the various
readings selected as background for each year's Commencement
farewell often speak in different "voices"—even though they
come from the same person. That, I think, is unavoidable. Few
roles in our society contain a larger set of responsibilities to different constituencies than that of university president. Different
styles of address are customary in different venues; formality is
both more appreciated and better understood by faculty, for example, than it is by students. I hope that the transitions, always
more abrupt when anthologized than they were in real life, will
not prove jarring.

CHAPTER ONE

Beginning

1980–1981

In the fall of 1980, Stanford held the usual kind of inauguration ceremony for its eighth President. It was held in the lovely outdoor setting of Frost Amphitheater; and although it was preceded by the customary procession of visiting and local academic figures, it had a delightfully informal flavor. Attended mostly by faculty and staff, augmented by a few idly curious undergraduates, it was a chance for the new President to set out his hopes for the university under his leadership.

That was and is a risky business. Yogi Berra is credited with having said, though he almost certainly did not, that "prediction is difficult, especially when you're talking about the future." And in the announcement of goals and ambitions, hopes are immediately converted by listeners into firm expectations. Investitures are thus good occasions for the construction of petards with which one may later be hoisted. (My predecessor, Dick Lyman, ruefully remembers that on his inauguration he told a reporter—in response to a question—that he expected to serve for about ten years. He learned about tickler files: in his last year he was frequently asked by the media when, exactly, he expected to step down.)

It seemed plain to me that I had to be explicit about two goals: the need to correct a kind of endemic imbalance at Stanford that had seemed to condemn the humanistic disciplines to a place behind the sciences; and the challenge of rebuilding the relationship between faculty and students, which had been altered by the traumas of the 1960s and was under threat from rapidly escalating research pressures. From the choice of these goals and the talk itself, it is clear that a central concern was for the quality of undergraduate education. That stayed at the top of my list for my entire term, and I returned to it more forcefully in the last two years.

In the inaugural statement it seemed important to begin with the common ground, by analyzing the resonance between people and institutional tradition that characterizes the best academic communities. I had then, and still have, a conviction that leadership is not a process through which one person pulls and others follow. Organizations move because they share a sense of purpose, and agree on a destination. Most effective leaders, I thought—and I certainly yearned to be one—seemed able to reflect this consensus repeatedly, in a way that reminds everyone where they're headed.

"It is difficult to analyze the bonds that tie one so firmly and meaningfully to an institution; yet they are worth serious study, because the feelings of commitment they generate provide much of the strength that resides in communities.

"What makes the subject complex is that we know no more about institutional character than we know about national character. Obviously members *share* certain characteristics, which they owe to the circumstances of their gathering and to their subsequent history. But is there, in addition, some emergent property that makes an institution special in a lasting way? Do tradition and custom evoke responses from members that they would not give elsewhere? And do these responses, translated as commitments, then add a self-sustaining element to the institutional character that inspired them, endowing the latter with a life of its own? That is *not* an easy notion to accept, particularly for universities—where whatever institutional character there is must be reasserted and reconfirmed, generation after short generation.

"Yet I *believe* in the transcendent character of institutions, and I believe I understand how it happens. It results from careful, conscious choices. That character becomes a self-fulfilling prophecy as people who like it affiliate, and then find their allegiance claimed. In this way we deliberately subscribe to values more durable than ourselves—and in doing so we help perpetuate them. What has this process of coadaptation produced that is particular to Stanford?

"The first element is distinctively Western and distinctively self-sufficient, and it comes out of the earliest roots of the University. Hard though it may now be to imagine, this campus at the time of its beginnings must have been—to its pioneer intellectual community from Ithaca and Cambridge and Bloomington—an isolated and even a hazardous place. In the memorable introduction to *The Sound of Mountain Water*, Wally Stegner reminds us that the West was an oasis society. His colleague Albert Guerard recalls that his father gave a similar feeling of the character of the campus in 1907: 'With the background of the tawny hills and the bluish range beyond . . . we had the sense of being in an oasis; we could almost feel the hot breath of the desert.' Small wonder that the undergraduate men of that day referred to themselves as 'roughs.' By contrast, the campuses of the Eastern private universities must have seemed intensely urban, or coolly pastoral.

"That element combines with another, harder to define but also probably related to *place*, to make an important imprint upon the character of the University. A strong early attachment to the natural and the practical sciences was blended with the traditional respect for the classical disciplines of the liberal arts. David Starr Jordan was a biologist; and his academic tradition was not that of Harvard but of Cornell, where agriculture and engineering existed side-by-side with classics and philosophy. This marriage of utility and culture, so clearly right for the sparsely settled West, has yielded one of the very few institutions in which education in the arts and sciences, including the applied sciences and the professions, are all pursued according to the highest standards. (That early utilitarian interest, though it reluctantly left agriculture to the land-grant institutions, produced among other early accomplishments the West's first station for the study of marine biology, and the beginnings of one of the world's great engineering schools.)

"The tradition woven of these beginnings is one that simultaneously admits the strength and excellence of the scholastic, and the freshness and vigor of the practical. Thus, strands that we might characterize as Eastern and Western have yielded a distinctive institutional fabric on which rich academic messages are conveyed through cheerful design. The style is relaxed and unpretentious, even to the point of looking less than intellectual to uncomprehending or unfriendly critics. (They miss our strength in that analysis—but we ought to be warned, that although discomfort is not a necessary condition for academic achievement, too much enjoyment *can* be distracting.)

"Above all, perhaps from its Western beginnings, there is a strong streak of individuality. Though Stanford *is*, in the main, a friendly, decent place in which people care about each other, a dominant characteristic is its individualism and an accompanying respect for personal independence. And Stanford has been unusually open to outside influence, and unpersuaded that it alone can confer merit. That helps to immunize us against self-satisfaction—the worst risk of being good at what one does.

"Our openness, furthermore, has yielded an unusual degree of intellectual democracy—a respect for the individual that permits affiliation across wide gulfs of age or particular knowledge and, more remarkably, across intellectual boundaries that in many other places are defended with territorial ferocity.

"The final aspect of our character I want to explore has to do with growth, and increases in complexity. The large university is a relatively recent phenomenon: Harvard was 250 years old before it had a senior class of 100, and as late as 1920 only one

U.S. university—the University of California at Berkeley—had a five-figure enrollment. In the expansion period between the two world wars, Stanford developed only modestly; its big surge was deferred until the great accomplishments of the Sterling years. The kinetics of that growth were not primarily related to trends in student enrollment; rather, they were governed by a law that I suspect affects the growth of all knowledge-producing enterprises: the more you know, the harder and more expensive it is to know the next thing.

"Stanford's growth spurt was an integral part of intellectual revolutions in the physical sciences, the biomedical sciences, and the information sciences. Every major area of development in these three revolutions—lasers, accelerators, the genetic code, perception theory, semiconductors, recombinant DNA—has had vital contributions from the extraordinary flowering of scientific productivity at Stanford. These are the ultimate products of the marriage between the Eastern intellectual tradition and earthy Western pragmatism that had earlier animated the founding years of the University.

"These recent events, like the earlier ones, have significantly shaped what Stanford is. There is a disparity of emphasis—not overwhelming to be sure, but still there—between the sciences and the humanities. There has also been a relatively recent expansion in scale primarily related to research, and thus involving parts of the institution that are not particularly close to many students. Both the emphasis problem and the size problem are challenges to us.

"The first of these challenges—the building of the humanities—is a straightforward and welcome task. It requires only a candid assessment of our needs and a vigorous effort to meet them. The deficiencies of library resources that previously inhibited our efforts have been substantially corrected in the Lyman years. Now we must add to the faculty strength we have already built, and we must create new institutional opportunities for Stanford's scholars in humanistic studies to work together and with visitors.

"The second challenge—how to accommodate the increased size and complexity demanded by our research programs and still be true to our character as a teaching institution—will be more formidable. I think we will need to remind ourselves again and again of Stanford's special knack. We have always been a little lean, and have made up for it by stretching our individual capacity and range. We have asked a great deal of ourselves and of our students, but—and this is the knack—we have made a collaborative venture of it. We have recognized that students, particularly the extraordinary students who gather here, teach some things to one another in their university years that their faculty cannot teach; and we have taken more seriously than most the role of catalyst—that is, of reliance upon stimulated rather than superintended learning. That is our tradition, and it has yielded a university college of special character. But I nevertheless find it, at the beginning of the 1980s, falling short of its potential. The fragile relationship between students and faculty, so critical to this *modus vivendi*, experienced serious damage in the late 1960s and early 1970s. The damage is not irremediable; but it needs attention. It arises from two sources.

"First, the years of the late 1960s were difficult and troubling ones for the people of my profession and my generation. Many of us originally chose careers in university teaching in part because they offered propinquity to the young (and perhaps, thereby, the continuous opportunity of rejuvenation!).

"But other, later, memories are not so pleasant—as we all know. There were profoundly alienating differences in the late 1960s—largely differences of view, not about policy ends, but about the propriety of pursuing them through means that violated other institutional values. As if that were not enough shock for a faculty accustomed to affection, it was made abundantly clear that its students no longer wished the University to stand *in loco parentis*. There was—or seemed to be—a denial that the University should have any relationship to students other than as generator and purveyor of information, or occasionally as landlord, preferably absentee.

"I happen to think the message was misread: It was not, in most cases, a plea for distance but instead an appeal for the reformulation of a relationship. But in the rhetoric of the time, the rejection of certain values of the prevailing adult culture came to sound like a rebellion against all adult attention. As a result, many things changed. It became, for example, much harder to get the average 40-year-old professor to sit down comfortably with a group of 20-year-olds at a luncheon table. The events of the 1960s left relatively untouched the fellowship of the laboratory bench, the dissertation conference, and the review journal. But faculty participation in residential education, in advising, and in more casual voluntary relationships with students—these were frequent casualties.

"So whether or not the message was misunderstood at the time, the alienation was real enough. And it is scarcely surprising that the young have recovered from it, whereas their elders have not. Their life cycles in the institution are, after all, very different. Since 1970, two-and-a-half student generations have come and gone, whereas over half of us here now on the faculty were also here then. There is thus a disparity between the readiness of students and of faculty to *perceive*, let along to correct, the problem.

"The second source of damage to undergraduate education was quite different. The growth spurt through the 1960s, to which I already referred, also saw a major reorganization of the opportunities afforded faculty members. Increases in sponsored research brought greater emphasis on kinds of scholarly work usually done without the involvement of undergraduate students. And new attention was paid to new forms of education and to new clienteles: post-doctoral fellows, residents, and so on. Now, there is nothing wrong with these changes; the new activities are perfectly proper parts of our enterprise. But at a time of disenchantment with what used to be our main concern, they became not merely legitimate but almost unfairly attractive avenues of faculty withdrawal.

"These two developments have hurt us. We have asked a great deal of a faculty that is thinner, in relation to its responsibilities, than that of most comparable universities; and the cost of the changes I have described has consequently been heavy. The challenge before us amounts to nothing less than the reformation of undergraduate education, yet I do not see how we can make much serious progress with it until we can evaporate the aftermath of mistrust that has hung over us for so long. From the personal observations of our most thoughtful students and faculty, and the comments of our sternest critics, we are told that our main failures lie in the area of faculty attention to the particular, individual needs of students: academic advising, thoughtful criticism of ideas, counseling, and the rendering of editorial judgment.

"The reformation of undergraduate education is not, at first glance, promising territory for the exercise of academic leadership. And we should understand, going in, that the degree of difficulty is high: all the Presidents, Provosts, Deans and Department Chairs together cannot dragoon harassed men and women into finding a twenty-fifth hour in the day for personal counseling. But I want to urge my faculty colleagues here today that it is time to assert that these activities matter, for the same reasons that classroom teaching and other, more traditional elements of academic responsibility matter. We are a residential university for the very good reason that there is a close linkage between what goes on in the classroom and what goes on in the lives students lead outside the classroom. We cannot refuse to engage with life off the Quad. In particular, we cannot refuse to do so merely because once, a long time ago, students may have told us that they didn't expect us to be their parents. We are not that, and never were. But we have become discouraged even about being mentors, and that is not right.

"Not only can we venture to carry academic programs into the rest of students' lives; we ought, in addition, not hesitate to deal forthrightly with such difficult matters as tolerance, how people live together, how they plan their futures, and what they expect of us. Students will respect what we are and do, not just what we say; that is why we must reflect, in our own policies and actions, the values we hope to communicate. Matters ranging from faculty affirmative action to support of the Honor Code take on an importance beyond their soundness as policies; they are examples of what we think is right. We need not hesitate to close with these issues. The way is open; the walls that were put up a decade ago have crumbled around us. All we need do is take a few bold steps away from the wreckage.

"For *all* of us, the greatest challenge is how to give these ambitions programmatic embodiment—how to lift ourselves above merely rhetorical solutions. We have begun by trying to improve the environments in which instruction takes place—not a trivial matter—and to put new emphasis on the advising program and on residential education. The kind of collaboration we get from students in this effort was strikingly illustrated by this year's pre-registration, orientation, and advising activities for new students: The number of returning students who came back early to Stanford to play official roles was over 400. What more dramatic statement could there be that students care about the climate of learning?

"I also plan to make continual use of a cabinet on undergraduate education that will consist of Deans, Administrators, Chairs of faculty committees, and student representatives. With this group I hope we can develop, over this year, specific plans for improving our performance, and I shall be responsible for finding the resources to carry them out.

"I feel confident about the outcome of all these efforts because I know you, know how you feel about this place, and know how much you have done for it. But something also needs to be said about leadership, and I shall conclude with that.

"The traditions of which I have spoken are strong, and the web of its intellectual and human relationships durable. Great universities have survived periods of indifferent leadership—even rather long ones. Nor can a president, however ambitious, lift an institution far if it lacks the internal fabric I described.

These observations suggest that we might be able to do without strong leadership—that we could get along with the kind of technician who manages what is already there, regularly accomplishes the probable, and seldom attempts the unlikely.

"I suppose I might accept that prescription, perhaps even with a moderate sense of relief, except that it is so incompatible with another Stanford tradition—one directly illustrated by the two men on the platform with me this afternoon. My predecessors leave for us the clearest possible illustration that leadership is more than management, that a President must do much more than maintain structure and conserve momentum.

"More how? *More*, I think, by leading the advocacy of the institution's own values, by reminding its members when there is a shortfall in living up to them, and by stimulating and supporting programs that give them higher expression; *more*, by helping in the constant work of constructing the institution's own value system, driving out the worst to make room for the best; *more*, by insisting that more often than not, the past and the future deserve equal consideration with the present.

"In the end leadership works best—indeed, may work only—when it is closely faithful to the institution's own character. Our Western legacy of friendly pragmatism makes us a community in which performance is valued along with analysis. Our Eastern inheritance reminds us of our need to reassert the primacy of intellectual accomplishment. Together they make us special in a way I am determined not to forget. Nor do I propose to let *you* forget it—for I promise you a period in which we will be aggressively ambitious for this splendid institution, and in which I will ask you—*all* of you—for support and help, again and again. Thank you."

The academic year itself was fascinating, intense, and anything but peaceful. I learned as much as I could, as quickly as I could. There was double-digit inflation, and budgeting was even more confusing than usual; a new Administration in Washington was in place, leading to doubts about the firmness of federal research support—doubts that matured into fear as the research universities protested severe proposed cuts in graduate student aid. I appointed a new Vice President for Medical Affairs, and a new Provost. We had controversies over an effort to unionize the clerical workers on campus, and developing concerns over the commercialization of research, especially in biotechnology. I found myself wishing that I had had more than one year as Provost under Dick Lyman's able mentorship before moving across the hall into his old office. Thus, for the most part, it was a year of frenetic self-education—and of getting to know the new constituencies of alumni, donors, and Trustees.

Commencement time came quickly that year. Those who know Stanford well know that the events of graduation present an opportunity for the emergence of a certain whimsical disorder—an institutional custom most publicly represented by the Incomparable Leland Stanford Junior University Marching Band. (This group of pranksters considers marching as evidence of paramilitary leanings, and will have none of it. Their specialties are scramble formations, big-band rock 'n' roll, and political satire, and their muse is, as mathematician/musical comedian Tom Lehrer once said of his own, not fettered by such inhibitions as taste. These preferences do not always endear them to alumni.)

One of the first events of Commencement weekend is a plaque-laying ceremony, in which the seniors remove a tile from the Inner Quad walkway and replace it with a bronze plaque containing their class numerals. The excavation beneath is filled, as part of the ceremony, with various class memorabilia and other contemporariana; the idea is to disinter it on an unspecified future date. The mood is not exactly serious.

It is customary for the Provost to address this event, and in 1980 I decided to deliver a homily about the impermanence of knowledge. This has served as the basis for many subsequent analyses, and it is useful here because it says something about the temper and mood of Commencement at Stanford.

"The custom we observe today—of having each class place its numerals in the floor of the inner quadrangle—was originated by the men and women of the Stanford class of 1896. Their class plate lies directly in front of the steps leading into the Memorial Church. It is a unique property of the digits 9 and 6 that they have mirror symmetry, so that they give the same year whether you are leaving the church or entering it! History does *not* record whether the Class of '96 understood this property of the two digits and exploited it.

"That may be just as well, because on this subject history can be misleading. As a new Provost approaching this occasion, I asked for background. The Office of Public Affairs was prepared to provide it: they gave me a standard text that several previous Provosts have used. In it there appeared a remarkable statement by Jordan about the length of the Inner Quad, which caused me to do an early morning measurement, and then develop the following talk—which begins with the statement itself. 'We are indebted to Stanford's first President, Dr. David Starr Jordan, for an estimate he made in 1896: namely, that it would be the year 2517 when the plaques would complete the perimeter "once around the Quad." . . . Dr. Jordan also estimated that the four adjacent series of red and brown squares could also be filled—one year at a time—to carry us comfortably to June 12, 5097.'

"I read those predictions on a nice day, and so I did a little fieldwork by counting the red tiles in the center row that are replaced each year by the Class Plaque. There are 185 in each of the long arcades, and 71 in each of the short arcades, for a total of 512. Eighty-eight of these have already been occupied by the plaques of your predecessors, starting the '92 in square one. That sequence will end when the plaque of the class of 2403 is placed in square 512. To say it quickly and get it over with, Dr. Jordan was off by 114 years, or squares—about a 22 percent error. But it isn't easy. The *Daily* got it wrong, too—by 23 years. And I got it wrong by two until Bob Beyers caught the error in a draft of this speech.

"We cannot exonerate Jordan by assuming that he has been the victim of a copying error, or that Public Affairs merely invented the number; the Stanford *Daily* (then called the *Daily Palo Alto*) of May 26, 1897, quotes him at length.

"A more apocalyptic hypothesis also occurred to me: the number of tile-spaces was abruptly reduced by the 1906 earthquake. It can be rejected, unfortunately, because Dr. Jordan's computation is also in error about the date at which the four adjacent rows will be filled—and in error by a different amount. I also considered whether Jordan might have extended the line of tiles out to Outer Quad at the corners, but that would yield an error in the other direction.

"So, alas, I must leave you with a scientific—or possibly an historical—mystery to ponder. One aspect of the case, however, is *not* mysterious. Previous Provosts of the University have recited those figures on this occasion without announcing that they are in error. I scarcely know what to say about this except to take it as a tribute to their tact. My guess is that each one stole onto the Quad, just as I did, early upon a morning; that each made his secret count of the spaces; and that each gasped at the discovery that Stanford's first president, one of the world's great systematic zoologists, appeared to have had difficulty with arithmetic. It falls to me—like Jordan, a biologist and even a recreational ichthyologist—to break this conspiracy of silence and reveal to you that it will only be 423 instead of 537 years before we fill the Inner Quad with class plaques.

"I hope you will find this knowledge to be an appropriate statement about the life and work of the University. On the one hand, we get from the stately progress of these bronze class footsteps a sense of the stabilizing influence of this great institution on human culture. And—through the sudden discovery that it is not *quite* so stately as we thought—we gain a renewed sense of the dynamism of knowledge, and the ephemerality of conviction."

Commencement itself was an opportunity to engage a problem that had increasingly troubled me during the academic year. In every public venue, the undergraduates of that day were being decried as careerists, uninterested in either serious intellectual engagement or—perhaps even worse—societal improvement.

Now, presidents sometimes get a little out of touch with the student body. Knowing that, I had taken on some freshman advisees and committed myself to about two dozen appearances for talks or question-and-answer sessions in undergraduate residences during the academic year; and I thought I knew better. My colleague Herant Katchadourian, with John Boli, had begun a major research project on student attitudes, later published as *Careerism and Intellectualism Among College Students*. They were developing a typology of Stanford undergraduates that included some careerists all right, but put them very much in the minority. And my own experience told me that given the right opportunity, our students were making extraordinarily generous social commitments, not only off the campus but to one another.

So a major theme of my graduation farewell that year was to point out some of the ways in which broader societal influences and choices had limited their options, and also contributed to this negative stereotyping. I also tried to point the way toward institutional initiatives that might provide new opportunities—a notion that led, a few years later, to the establishment of the Haas Public Service Center at Stanford. Talking about the importance of public service on the occasion itself was natural, because the main speaker was Warren Christopher, J.D. '49—a Stanford trustee recently returned from government, where he had successfully negotiated the release of U.S. hostages in Iran. Much later, of course, he cycled back to government for a third time, as Secretary of State in the Clinton administration.

The beginning of the farewell talk is spiced with some references to Stanford institutions and to my own earlier history. The Dean Fred of the introduction was an uncommonly successful and admired Director of Admissions at Stanford from 1969 to 1984; he subsequently went to the College Board and then to the deanship at Princeton. Branner Hall, once a women's dormitory, is the largest all-Frosh residence at Stanford. It is noted for its frenetic energy level; in one memorable description, Branner

students were called "hyper but clueless" by a haughty sophomore. And Manzanita is a group of trailers, which by this time
had become the least desirable undergraduate housing assignment. When they were new in the late 1960s they were thought
to be temporary, and were highly regarded. But, as their T-shirt
proclaimed, Stanford's "Adult luxury mobile home community"
eventually demonstrated that "there is nothing so permanent as
temporary housing."

*It is now my right and privilege to engage the graduates as a
captive audience for their last time. But of course it is also my
first time, and therefore a doubly special occasion. I shall
briefly examine, according to our custom, the timeless question:
"Is There Life After Stanford?"*

*There is no better time than Commencement to reflect on the
cyclicity of life in an institution like this one. At the time the
class of 1981 was opening its acceptance letters from Dean Fred
I was taking leave of my Human Biology class to go to Washington and try to run a regulatory agency that had just decided
to take your diet soda away. And now, as you complete your
senior year—still, I must note, drinking Tab among other
things—I am finishing up as a freshman President.*

*There may be more to this metaphor than you now suspect; I
sometimes catch myself wondering whether, having experienced
a first-year high roughly equivalent to that of Branner Hall, I
am not about to be deposited, as by some midlife version of the
Sophomore Slump, in the Manzanita trailers. It has been a good
first year, largely because my predecessor gave me a splendid
start and because this place is so supportive. But as we all know,
the future has in it more than a few portents of Slump: there is,
for example, the Economy, and then there is the Cure for the
Economy.*

*Other portents, no doubt, are on your minds—or will be, as
they turn from reflections on the past to examination of the future. To begin with, I wonder what you think of all the charac-
terizations of your college generation's approach to that future?*

The mass psychoanalysis of college students has always been a popular indoor sport, but now it is downright trendy. One commentator after another has aggregated you and overgeneralized you, and shoved you in a pigeonhole labeled "careerist." For a sample I give you the following from a recent book by one Landon Jones, Senior Editor of People *magazine (where else would one go for the least common denominator of conventional wisdom?) Jones puts it right on the line: "Today's students are passive, conformist and materialistic. They care about jobs, while the baby boomers (their predecessors of ten years ago) cared about life."*

I find that superficial. It would be surprising if our economic ills did not have more people thinking and talking about the security of their futures—but that is not proof of a corresponding loss of idealism. In fact, I regularly advertise you to my contemporaries as being, below the surface, as concerned with the state of the world and your fellows as your predecessors. The criticism you are hearing from most analysts of your generation is, I think, a form of projection. They would rather blame the failures of service in our society on the choices you make than on the quality of opportunity they have provided.

What do I mean by failures of service? They are all around us.

For example: the quality of public education is declining, and especially sharply in unexpected places, like California. Not only are indices of student performance like average SAT scores falling steadily; so, more disturbingly, is the quality of people entering the teaching profession. Last year, the mean SAT scores of college-bound high school seniors intending to teach was 35 points below the national average for all college-bound high school seniors.

For example: government service at State and Federal levels is increasingly unattractive, as judged by the number of well-prepared college graduates choosing to enter it.

For example: we are a nation with more than enough physicians by any aggregate standard, but we cannot manage a dis-

tribution of those physicians equitable enough to permit Black and Hispanic people in our cities, or the rural poor, anything like the access to health care enjoyed by most people in the United States.

It is easy to blame these problems on you who are making the choices. We hear things like these: "the young these days aren't concerned about public service"; "medical school graduates are going where the rich are"; and "they're only interested in college as a route to job security."

That is too easy. It was not the young who structured these career incentives. They did not defeat the school board measures, or pass the Proposition 13's and 2½'s. Adult property owners did that. They did not, in the course of two successive campaigns, blame most of our social ills on hardworking civil servants, whom they contemptuously called "bureaucrats." Adult candidates for the Presidency and the Senate did that. They did not make it necessary for medical students to finance their training by assuming crushing debt loads that can scarcely help but limit their options for service; adult politicians and health policy-makers did that.

As if these disincentives to public service were not discouraging enough, there is a second problem. Having once engaged in the effort to engineer social improvement, having perhaps overdone it, and having noted some prominent failures, too many among us are now prepared to conclude that social improvement cannot be sought through social effort.

For example, "busing is a failure," say the same social scientists who once advocated it—proving this point, by the way, using the same kind of analysis with which they reached the opposite conclusion the first time around. And "the environmental movement has brought us an energy crisis," say others—or, on their bumper stickers, "Let the Sierra Club freeze in the dark."

These claims reflect a kind of conspiracy to ignore some extraordinary successes produced by the great movements of the 1960s. The largest proportion of our people in history have been brought through secondary school; trout and salmon swim in waterways that had been dead for decades, like the Connecticut River and Lake Erie; you and I can see Mt. Diablo on most days; a person confined to a wheelchair can, with courage, successfully complete college. And even a former white supremacist in Louisiana, quoted by Robert Coles, can say: "I never would have dreamed back in 1960 that we'd come to this—the black people holding their heads up as high as ours, everywhere you go in this town. . . . We couldn't think of going back to the old days." These are momentous human triumphs. Rather than deny them, we should note them with pride.

Even if it is true that the social interventions of the 1960s have been less successful than we once hoped, does that justify a retreat from idealism? A suspension of belief in the efficacy of social service? I think that would be an overreaction to disappointment. We Americans are disposed to have too much faith in the quick technological fix—to expect repairs to "take" instantly. Our view of past efforts to reshape society is skewed by that kind of overexpectation. That brings me to a point about your own education. Exactly this same sort of disproportionate faith in new technology is present now, in a different and much more pernicious form; and I suspect it is a part of a more general loss of belief in social obligation. We are in danger of a national infatuation with the efficacy of utilitarian analysis— cost/benefit ratios, trade-offs, and the rest. Here at Stanford we teach such stuff in half a dozen public policy courses, and although it's useful within limits, I have the uneasy feeling that some of the people whizzing through the calculations may not have read Locke, Rousseau, or Mill, and may not quite understand that a framework of social justice theory should always underlie and often limit that mode of analysis. We need to know who benefits, who pays the costs, and whether the arrangements coincide with our basic notions of fairness. In short, at the heart of the matter are some values—values that emerge from our history, our traditions, our social experience: the classic subject matter of liberal learning.

This general sense of cart-before-horse has made me something of a fundamentalist about undergraduate education here. The phrase I would take for a theme is "beyond utility." To balance our preoccupation with systems, to remind us that analysis isn't everything, we need a humanistic vision. That vision includes the values and convictions that underlie all of the more utilitarian, more professional, more technique-oriented things we have to spend so much time learning to do. And that vision subtends much of the rest of what is called, in an old-fashioned way, education, as opposed to training.

I have moved from the public characterization of your generation's motives to some observations about your education. From these, I wish to glean for you two pieces of advice. Would you, after all, feel complete on this day without some advice you didn't ask for?

The first is not to let others tell you what you're thinking about, or how worried about your future you seem to be, or how undedicated to service. There are abundant opportunities to make the world better. They may not be as attractive as they should be—but they are there and you can seize them. I hope many of you will. Public service matters: and one person can make a difference. You have just heard from the living proof (Warren Christopher).

The second is to pursue, and urge your children and your university to pursue, learning that is beyond utility. I do not know what future reflections you will have on your own education, but I bet that some of you, after some fumbling around, will find yourselves in a position like this: your background knowledge and technical ability are just right for a job; in short it's a good fit, and what we might call your training has stood you in good stead. Then—just then—is when your education will start to be important to you.

I wish for each of you a life that will contain many realized opportunities for service, animated by revelations that reach beyond utility.

And I thank you for this year.

CHAPTER TWO

Speaking Out

1981–1982

In my second year in office, I had begun to recognize both the necessity and the hazard of taking public positions on issues affecting the University. Concern over the growth of commercial influences on research, particularly biomedical research, was increasing. Early in the year, I testified before Congress on proposed cuts in federal support of graduate education, and soon afterward, I found myself leading a protest in the higher education community against government policies intended to restrict the access of foreign visitors to basic research laboratories.

Although none of these issues particularly stirred the undergraduate student body, I began to realize that on other matters I was expected to be a spokesperson for one view or another. Organizations devoted to a particular good work or policy came occasionally to suggest that I "take a position" on their issue. Sometimes, furthermore, I was tempted to do so!

I suspect that every university president, early in his or her term, has to come to grips with this. Too much public posturing is bad. So is too much caution: a lengthy *New York Times* article decries the silence of academic leaders on important public issues. It even reports that the Stanford trustees warned my successor about being too public, in view of the "outspoken, controversial" record of his predecessor!

That is actually not an implausible claim. I probably was somewhat too outspoken, and certainly Trustees become acutely uncomfortable when their institution is mentioned too often in the newspapers. But presidents do have to represent the institution in representations to the outside world—and it is important to reach an understanding about which statements represent "the university." So I tried to develop some criteria about speaking out—and at the end of that essay, I tried to deal with the various versions of "the university" and what voice represents it.

"Finally, something needs to be said about statements made explicitly on behalf of the University. This matter has attracted recent comment in connection with two particular issues: the testimony offered by the University on State retirement age legislation proposals in 1979, and the position we took regarding the effort to organize office workers and library support staff this past Spring. In each instance, it was argued by some that it was inappropriate to attribute to 'the University' positions taken by its senior officers on particular matters. Rather, it was asserted, those positions ought to be identified as those of 'the Administration,' in order to differentiate them from others on which there is a consensus among the various constituencies of the University.

"To begin with, although many of us speak of the University as a community—and hope fervently that it continues to be one—the University is also a legal entity. It is this latter version of the University with which the outside world interacts formally, at least much of the time. It is this official University that admits students, graduates them, certifies their academic performance, raises some monies, expends others, responds to government and to citizens, and sues or is sued when those responses go badly. It is thus not unreasonable to expect that when positions are articulated on behalf of 'the University,' they actually represent that entity to which others will assume we refer.

"Some may view this as a rather strict construction. I would point out, however, that it does *not* leave 'the senior officers' of the University as the sole spokespersons for the institution. On the contrary, the faculty—and the student body—have well-defined zones of responsibility within which they, and not administrative officers, are entitled to speak with the official voice of the University.

"Changes in the curriculum, requirements for degrees, the appointment and promotion of faculty, and other academic policy decisions are made (or at least initiated) by the faculty. In these areas, it is perfectly legitimate for the faculty collectively to represent its views as the University's, just as it is for the senior administrative officers to represent theirs as the University's when, for example, a matter of compensation policy is under discussion. Thus this strict formulation does not set the administrative officers of the University above other constituencies. It simply reflects a separation of powers, with which we are all familiar, that permits each constituency to represent the University when it has the authority to do so.

"There may well be other occasions on which we wish to refer to the University loosely as a community, rather than as a legal entity. When we are doing that, we should probably state as 'University' positions only those that emerge from a firm consensus. But I think we should all be warned that this is difficult territory: first, because the more rigorous definition of the University is the more widely understood and the more explicit, so that we risk confusion in the looser usage; and second, because there is no commonly understood standard for establishing how much consensus would be required for a 'University' position under these terms. A group of faculty opposing some administrative action, for example, might insist that unless there is near unanimity in favor of it among the faculty, a consensus cannot be said to exist. And what, then, of students? And staff? Alumni also hold a stake in the institution, and so do donors. Do these groups also have a right to participate in the establishment of this version of the University's position? If so, I'm afraid it is a version destined to slide rapidly toward paralysis.

"This last point brings me around to a larger question, one often ignored in discussions of who speaks for the University. It has to do with *why* the legal entity of the University has the structure it does. There is one important respect in which the University-as-community notion fails, and fails seriously. It is this: the 'community' of which everyone speaks is actually *the community of the present*. The *legal* entity of the University, though it may seem narrower than this, is actually broader, because it entails the vision of the University as the community of the present *and of all possible futures*. The guardians of this version of the institution have responsibility not only for what is, but for what is to become—the unappointed faculty, the unmade experiment, the unborn student. The difficulty with all communities of the present is that, again and again, they behave in ways that show too much preference for the present and too much discount for the future. The whole notion of trusteeship and of fiduciary responsibility, in which the legal version of the university is rooted, is designed to counterbalance this incentive. I am always amazed at how many people in university communities-of-the-present misunderstand this point. They suppose that Trustees are there to provide disinterested guidance, or external accountability, or a "good business head," or stern oversight, or new resources. Trustees give us, from time to time, each of the above, but that is not their central function. That central function is to speak for the future against a chorus of voices that lay claim to the present.

"I think it not unlikely that, at one time or another, the President will have to adopt a position that goes quite *against* the consensus of the community-of-the-present. Could such a statement ever be, legitimately, a University position? I believe it could, because the President has the obligation to represent not merely the rights of those who are there, but all of those who have not yet arrived. It is that comprehensive, equilibrium view of the institution to which I think we should apply the full, formal force of the phrase *the University*. And it is logically closer, I think, to the legal definition than it is to the community-of-the-present."

One of the issues I thought worth speaking out on—and sufficiently generic to avoid most of the self-denying ordinances I set out earlier—was the increasingly pernicious trend toward single-issue, special-interest politics. It seemed equally applicable to the university community as to the polity more generally, and I treated it in this address to the Associated Students Speakers' Bureau.

"I think one of the things that is seriously wrong with our society is the degree of absolutism and moral certainty that everyone seems willing to assert. I am not aiming this at the 'Moral Majority' because, although I find them very unattractive, I do not consider them a particularly important target. Much more troubling, it seems to me, is the disease of which they are just one symptom: the triumph of single interests, single issues, single values.

"Everywhere one looks, these are being accorded more weight in national discourse. The forceful, often well-deserved successes of moral imperatives in the 1960s have become epidemic. Once primarily the property of the political Left, one-dimensional convictions have been enthusiastically embraced by the Right—a transfer perhaps officially celebrated by the strange migration of Libertarianism, which a few years ago bridged the far Left to the far Right, much as the color circle is closed through the extra-spectral purples. In addition to Libertarians and a self-styled Moral Majority, we have right-to-lifers and animal rights advocates and even a me-first movement. The particular values—some of which are not so terrible—are not important to my point. What *is* important is the willingness of the advocates to assign infinite weight to their particular value, and to discount all competing ones.

"A university education with a proper emphasis on liberal culture and the origins of thought ought to be an antidote. Of all the lessons it imparts, perhaps the most valuable is that human society is complex, and so is the matter of an individual's obligation to it. There is no one value; there are many, and frequently they collide, leaving us to weigh and to choose. It is the seductive character of the special interest that it seizes one value, and canonizes it. All arguments are thus conveniently converted from rational to theological discourse, and self-righteousness and intolerance are ascendant."

Athletic programs were an issue in 1981–82, too. A decade earlier, in response to widespread complaints from minority students and many, many others, President Richard Lyman had abolished the "Stanford Indian" as a mascot of the University's athletic teams. The Indian, itself a latecomer, had apparently been an invention of the great coach "Pop" Warner in the 1930s—brought with him from his previous engagement at the Carlisle Indian School. Part of the objection was based upon demeaning cartoon caricatures that were featured on many Stanford sports memorabilia. But even the putatively "noble" representations caused some problems. I remember that a thoughtful alumnus asked an American Indian student why he objected to the dances Prince Lightfoot performed on the football field with the Band; they were, after all, graceful and dignified. The student responded that the question itself demonstrated the difficulty. "You see something dignified and vaguely authentic. I see a Yurok Indian performing Plains dances in Navajo dress, and I find it troubling."

The demise of the Indian mascot left a void that various groups were quick to notice, and eager to fill. Among the nominees were the Griffons (a cultural favorite), Trees (the Band is still trying), and the Robber Barons. Stanford whimsy nearly won a victory for the last-named, but the nth referendum in 1981 produced a clear margin for the color Cardinal, period. I accepted this verdict, and issued these "instructions," tongue firmly in cheek:

"While various other mascots have been suggested and then allowed to wither, the color has continued to serve us well, as it has for 90 years. It is a rich and vivid metaphor for the very pulse of life. And it is, for Stanford, the historically correct symbol. Selected over gold in a vigorous dispute settled on the very afternoon of the first Big Game in 1892, it was the first word ever used in newspaper descriptions of a Stanford athletic victory: "Cardinal triumphs o'er Blue and Gold." Volume One of the *Quad*, in 1894, bears on its flyleaf the three symbols of the new University: its seal, a cheer consisting largely of iterations of "rah," and the single word CARDINAL.

"With this choice finally made, we find ourselves, as usual, unique in our own Conference, where one finds six mammals (all carnivores save one), a bird, a Sun Devil, and a military figure of some kind, but no other color. Colors do serve, however, as the sole symbol at some universities of distinction; moreover, well-chosen colors often come to dominate animal mascots when both are present.

"Cardinal is a color, and that is all it needs to be! We cannot actually prevent provincial sportswriters from lapsing into argot and calling us Birds, but we can certainly show our disapproval. Similarly, we cannot actually condemn those from less cultivated environments who mistakenly pluralize our color by referring to collectives of Stanford athletes as Cardinals. But we should instruct them, as considerately as possible, in the proper use of such nouns of venery. "Cardinal team" (or, if you must, "Card gridders," "Card netters," etc.) is acceptable; "Cardinals" or "Cards" bad usage. The *Daily* will no doubt be helpful in setting proper examples for the (dare I say it) less exacting outside media."

Athletic success at Stanford was building, and nowhere more impressively than in women's sports, where the university had gotten out ahead of Title IX and begun the development of what would become the nation's strongest intercollegiate program. The Senior Athletes' Dinner at the end of the academic year was the first in which both men's and women's sports were included, and it gave rise to some observations on that change and how it was a metaphor for other kinds of progress for women.

"I am reminded that there was a dinner like this in my own life, exactly thirty years ago. As a mediocre athlete at Harvard who tried three sports and managed to letter in one of them, I was entitled to attend the spring banquet of something that was actually called, believe it or not, The Harvard Varsity Club. It still is.

"There are some striking differences between that gathering and this one, but there is at least one similarity. That similarity is worth cherishing in an era of forged transcripts, unearned credits, phony transportation vouchers, and athletes who don't graduate. There were some pretty good athletes in that room, including the members of a crew that won the Henley Grand, but all of them were *students*. It is a continuing source of pride at Stanford that this is one of the places in which things are still that way.

"What about the differences? Perhaps the most obvious one is the presence, here, of some people who have two X-chromosomes. The Varsity Club dinner was notably lacking in women, who were not thought at the time to be 'much good at sports.' It occurs to me to wonder: what would the reaction have been if I had predicted that soon—before our thirtieth reunion, before our kids were all grown—women would run the Boston Marathon faster than it had ever been run by men up to that point? There would have been incredulous laughter from two-thirds of the room, accompanied by a little locker-room humor. The others—the intellectuals in the crowd—might have been willing to discuss the matter. This they would have done by supplying patient, thoughtful arguments about endurance differences, the shape of the pelvis, body fat proportions, the evolution of males as hunters and of females as gatherers, and other similar appeals to reason. But not a single person in the room would have regarded the prediction as one that should be seriously entertained.

"Yet that is just what has taken place. My classmates would be astonished at the happening, but they would be even more astonished at the trends. If we look at the past ten years of the world's best times in the marathon for men and women, it is clear that the women's mark has been dropping, over the decade, at a rate about seven times faster than the men's record. It could be argued that the women's record for the decade started at an artificially high value, because so few women were running the distance, and that the improvement was therefore 'easy.' If that were so, we'd expect most of the reduction to have taken place over the first half of the decade, that is, from 1971 to 1976. But in that period the record only dropped by 7:19—whereas from 1976 to 1981 it dropped by 13:42. In the corresponding five-year periods the men's record dropped by 1:13 and 1:42. Thus the *difference* between the men's and women's records has been more than cut in half in the last decade, and the *rate* of improvement of the women with respect to the men is twice as fast for the second half of the decade as it was for the first.

"An example from another sport may emphasize my point. In my senior year, Yale's swimming team held the national record for consecutive dual-meet victories, and had won the national intercollegiate championship twice. Harvard was also unbeaten in dual meets that year, and the confrontation at season's end, which Yale won to preserve its string, produced great interest— and some extraordinary times. What would have happened if you had put this year's Stanford women into that pool? (What, I mean, in addition to aquatic bedlam?) *Humiliation* is what.

"Just to give you a sample, seven current Stanford women would have beaten Dave Hedberg, Harvard's great sprint free-styler, and all the Yalies in the 100. The Stanford women would have swept the 200-yard backstroke and breaststroke, and won all the other events contested. In the 400-yard freestyle relay, there would have been a ten-second wait between Stanford's touch and the first man to arrive at the finish. Do you know how long ten seconds is? Can you imagine that crowd in Payne Whitney Gymnasium, seeing a team of *girls* line up against the two best freestyle relay groups in the East, expecting the expected, and then having to wait *this long*—for the men to get home? Suppose I had gotten up at the dinner in 1952 and put that scenario to them. Don't you think they would have called the health service for counseling?

"My point is a simple one. Even thoughtful, intelligent people—men, and a lot of women too—deeply believed that women had limitations of an inherent, biological kind that would prevent them from such accomplishments. Thirty, twenty, even fifteen years ago there was no debate over the existence of these limitations; instead, the discussions centered on what might account for them.

"And now, suddenly, we are discovering that we were absolutely dead wrong. The nice thing about the timed and measured sports in athletics is that the numbers are so decisive, and leave so little room for argument. What women's athletics are teaching us, I think, is that even the kindest and most thoughtful assessments of women's biological potential were hopeless underestimates.

"I ask you: If conventional wisdom about women's capacity can be so thoroughly decimated in this most traditional area of male superiority, how can we possibly cling to the illusions we have about them in other areas? What, in short, is the lesson to be drawn from the emerging athletic equality of women? I think it is that those who make all the other, less objectively verifiable assumptions about female limitations would do well to discard them. They belong in the same dusty closet with the notion that modern ballplayers couldn't carry Ty Cobb's spikes and the myth that blacks can't play quarterback. Whether it is vicious or incapacitating or merely quaint, nonsense is nonsense. And it dies hard."

My second year was also a year in which students, their education, and the ways in which Stanford supports both became part of the foreground in a new and forceful way. Need-based financial aid and other policies had enabled Stanford to diversify its student body considerably—a process that continued for the rest of the decade. This gradual change, welcome in so many ways, brought new issues to the student body, and to alumni as well.

For the students it meant dealing with difference in a much more demanding and intensive way. I tried to suggest some of the challenges as well as the rewards of meeting them in my welcome to the Class of 1985 in the Fall.

"So the first thing I would urge upon you is the need to overcome the limitations of your own background, whatever that may be, and eagerly confront other views, other convictions, other ways of doing things. I should warn you that this is not a painless process. It regularly produces some of the most difficult and trying moments in the lives of undergraduates here. But in the end, it is one of the most profoundly worthwhile and important things that can happen to you at Stanford.

"How to go about making it happen? I think the appropriate style is candid, aggressive exploration. You will notice that I have not used the word 'tolerance' to describe the attitude I think should exist between diverse segments of our student body. Tolerance is, under many circumstances, a virtue. Certainly it is preferable to intolerance. But it implies a kind of live-and-let-live view, one that confuses non-aggression with understanding. That is not what I am trying to recommend here; I am urging upon you something *beyond tolerance*: active exploration, risk-taking, exposure, a yearning to understand, and a willingness to change. To tolerate diversity is not what we aim for. We aim to celebrate it."

Stanford's increasing diversity also raised questions for some alumni. A few of them looked at our expanded programs of financial aid for needy students and our active recruitment of minority students, and wondered if the University hadn't taken on a giant project in social engineering. But one parent wrote me a wonderful letter about his scholarship-holding daughter's experience—at the end of which he apologized for not having been able to make a financial contribution to "repay" the university. It was a help to be able to explain, to him as well as to others, how "Sue" had already repaid Stanford for its investment. My reply formed a part of my annual report on the state of the University to the Academic Council in the spring.

"We shall be glad of your help, when and if you choose to give it. There is, however, one part of your formulation with which I would disagree. You'd like to help Stanford, you suggest, *because* of the aid your daughter has received. I hope I can convince you that you don't owe Stanford anything because of the aid Sue has received. Stanford's reward is her presence in the Class of 1985, and the dimension she adds to the diverse and talented group of undergraduates to which she belongs.

"Those qualities are what have convinced us that we *must* retain the policy that allowed us to admit Sue and her classmates in a fashion that was blind to their financial need—and then aid them to the full extent of their demonstrated need. As you and other parents well know, the formula that establishes what we shall give is not exactly lavish: we expect a lot of family 'stretching' and a lot of self-help. But we are prepared to do some stretching, too, and that is why we shall continue our commitment to a need-blind admissions policy.

"Why is this such an important institutional priority for us? The answer lies in our belief that students gain from one another a large fraction of what they take away from the college experience. If that is right, the composition of a student body, like the quality of the faculty and the equipment in the laboratories, is an essential part of the education we provide. Since the ability and diversity of the Stanford student body is an instrument of what we are trying to accomplish here, we invest in its quality just as we invest in the quality of the faculty. So Sue and the financial aid with which we provide her are part of the strategy. When it works well, as it has in her case, we share in your pride.

"These policies have never been more important than they are in this time of declining public investment in quality higher education. For reasons quite different from the ones I have set out above, the federal government has developed, over the past thirty years, programs that have helped guarantee educational access to young people of ability who lack financial resources. These programs have been based upon society's stake in the next generation of leadership, and on our national belief in equal opportunity. As the present administration abandons those commitments, the obligations of private institutions to shoulder part of the burden become even stronger.

"So I do hope for your support, now and in the future, and in various ways. But I would emphasize again that you do not need to repay us for Sue. She is doing that every day, by contributing to the vigor and diversity of this community and, in that way, to the growth of understanding that is its most significant outcome."

All this provided more than enough subtext for the 1982 farewell talk. There were other elements as well. My daughter Julia was a member of the graduating Class of 1982; plainly that required special effort. For the first time in memory, both the Baccalaureate and Commencement speakers were women: Stanford trustee Sandra Day O'Connor had been named, earlier in the year, as the first woman Associate Justice on the Supreme Court, and she gave the main address.

The themes of independence, confidence, and tolerance were central to the advice I gave Julia and her classmates in that year. I also thought it was important to remind them—especially in view of the public impression that they were career-driven automatons—of some nonacademic and nonoccupational aspects of their Stanford lives. Thus the farewell had a sentimental as well as a practical tone—a quality I thought might be forgiven in an about-to-be-abandoned father.

Now, Julia, and other friends of the Class of 1982, it is time to turn our attention to that ageless question: "Is There Life After Stanford?" I want to assure you that there is, and that it is good—better, in fact, than life before Stanford was, and better still than life without Stanford would have been. By this I mean that each of you will take away a special mixture of life-improving experiences and accomplishments from this period, and that as a consequence of these you will probably do more, and suffer less in doing it. Alternatively, you may do much more, and suffer anyhow. That's all right too.

Here are a few things that seem so important to me that I wish devoutly for their inclusion in your own collection of things gained at Stanford.

First, I hope you are aware that you think and analyze more confidently, and not just better. Perhaps the surest measure of intellectual capacity is the ability to do novel things with familiar tools. During a successful education, a sweeping new plateau comes into view with the realization that the tools one has been given actually work in the way they're supposed to when applied to unfamiliar materials. That experience provides liberation from the known, and permits survival voyages into the entirely unexplored—the original. The confidence bred of belief in one's own experience is a requirement for such voyages. I hope that each of you has come to know that experience during your time here, and thus to own the resulting confidence.

Second, I hope you can appreciate, and even seek, a wider range of beliefs, traditions, cultures and values than you would have welcomed otherwise. During your years at Stanford, there has been more than the usual amount of discussion about such matters. At least, I hope there has, because I have tried hard to help it along, out of a conviction that confronting difference is valuable, even (perhaps especially) when it is painful. That is why we have laid such great stress upon Stanford's diversity, as part of what we are and of what we offer educationally. And that is why we shall continue a relentless pursuit of that diversity, through admissions and financial aid policies, no matter how many others seem willing to abandon it. If the exposure has worked for you, then you understand its importance. If it has not, I hope at least you have the sense of having missed something significant, a sense that will prick your conscience to take up the search later on.

Third, I hope you may have gained one of the most useful byproducts of the educational process: a tolerance for ambiguity. Things are seldom certain in this world; living comfortably with that uncertainty (or, at least, living with it in the absence of acute misery) is a useful attribute to have. I say this with the *special conviction of one who would rather it were easier for him. . . .*

Fourth, I wish for you a related insight, which I shall call the multidimensionality of value. You will have encountered some extraordinarily able people in your time here, and many of them will have been deeply devoted to some value above all others: individual freedom, or world peace, or environmental quality, or the right to life, or equal opportunity. If you add up all the things they insist on, you will see that they cannot all be right; but neither is any one of them really wrong. That is because the great issues with which we grapple are seldom confrontations between good and evil; rather, they are collisions between competing goods. We cannot deal with such collisions except by doing the hard work to decide which, in a given situation, is more important. Because we cannot have all we want of each objective, we must make choices—and although the good-or-evil framework is quite unhelpful to us in making them, it is pushed at us insistently by people who are prepared to assign infinite worth to their own favorite value and to seek out and destroy all values in conflict with that one. I hope you have concluded that the more single-minded their conviction, the less attention they deserve.

Fifth, I wish for you a strong (but not incapacitating) skepticism about Certified Truth. Remember one of the great Stanford lessons: the textbook may be wrong, even if the professor teaching the course did write it. That is not a criticism of your professor, who is doubtless wonderful. But the impermanence of the written Word, the instability of conventional wisdom, is an important part of the intellectual dynamic in which I hope you will choose to live. In its way, this wish is the shadow of the first one. Confidence in your own capacity to analyze, interpret, project, experiment, reason includes the suspicion that They May Have it Wrong. A welcome emancipation from authority attaches to the realization that when the result of your own processes takes you into disagreement with what is written, it is entirely possible that you are correct.

Sixth, I hope you have gained esteem for the value of a sense of humor. Certainly this is a place in which laughter, whimsy, and even flat-out wackiness are alive and well. Remember that humor is no good if it isn't integrated; it can't be something you just turn to in the evening. It deserves a place in all of life, even in the most critical parts. As a matter of fact, you need it most when things seem least conducive to it. Like everyone else, I am busily constructing a set of personal "laws." One of Kennedy's first Laws will be the following: "If a belief is too serious to joke about, it's probably wrong."

And last but not least, I hope that in each of you there is a growing suspicion that it is not all that good to be cool. Enthusiastic commitment is risky, but so are a lot of worthwhile things. It is important not only to be able to engage with new ideas, but to be willing to make public declarations of your convictions without embarrassment and then to translate them into deeds. Oliver Wendell Holmes, Jr., made the definitive statement of that value, and it is worth quoting verbatim despite the then-characteristic defect that it omits one gender: "As life is action and passion," said Holmes, "it is required of a man that he should share the passion and action of his time at peril of being judged not to have lived."

Now, having gotten you out of here with these qualities— you'll note that you're confident, tolerant, wise, sophisticated, skeptical, witty, and unafraid—I want to ask you a favor in return. There are several things I wish you'd do before starting serious training for the '84 Olympics, shipping out on the Pacific steamer as a deckhand, marrying your hometown honey, and starting to read the Procedure casebook so you'll be a little ahead of the others. I know you'll want to get to these things right away. But first take a little time for the following agenda.

To begin with, thank some people. You've done that a good deal this week, I suspect, with family and friends here who have been supportive. Do it some more, and think about whom you may have forgotten. Let me suggest that one of them might be a teacher from your high school who made a difference to you at some critical point—who showed you that learning was worth the effort, and that you could do some things you didn't believe were within your reach. That person may well be more responsible than anyone here for your place in this event. Give her, or him, the special and unique joy that comes from knowing that what one did turned out later to be important. The rest of this society isn't doing its part for that teacher, so you'd better do yours.

Next, take time to reflect, and if possible to write, about some of the important things that happened to you here. Do so in the knowledge that nothing ends today; we have played our episodic part in what is an open, lifelong process. Possibly the most important contribution we can have made is to convince you of that open character of learning, and of the need to stay receptive.

Third, remember that we'd like to help with that. Stanford won't forget you. From time to time our reminders may sound more like appeals than invitations; forgive us that, and persevere in the knowledge that we care about you, and want to know how you're doing and how you feel about how we're doing.

Fourth, to help us in the latter effort, will you for God's sake fill out the Senior Survey?

And finally, will you now just take a look around you, and think about a few of the simple, untaxing pleasures that have enlivened your years here? It is perfectly OK that in addition to being an Intellectual Environment, Stanford is also a beautiful, friendly, vivid place. Give a thought to friendships, to idle times passed, to the green hills behind Lake Lag on an afternoon when breezy sunshine follows a March rain, to an unexpected surprise somebody arranged for you when you were a freshman, to the desert smell of the dry grass and eucalyptus on a hot October Saturday, to the best volleyball hit you ever got, to the dorm show, and to the extraordinary person you admired and then discovered was just as shy as you were. Reflect on these treasures, and store them, because sentiment matters.

A man unafraid of sentiment said these words to another graduating class in another place, many years ago. They are good parting words, and I leave you with them: "Your days are short here; this is the last of your springs. And now in the serenity and quiet of this lovely place, touch the depths of truth, feel the hem of Heaven. You will go away with old, good friends. And don't forget when you leave why you came."

CHAPTER THREE

Early Controversies

1982–1983

In the fall of 1982, Stanford students returned to a campus in the middle of a strike. By Registration Day, the members of United Stanford Workers had already been out for three weeks, and by the time a contract was finally agreed to in mid-October, the strike had become the longest work stoppage in the University's history. It was an uncomfortable time, and the fair but belated settlement left a significant cloud of dissatisfaction hanging over the beginning of the academic year.

Nor was that the only challenge. First among the others was a new issue over selective service. The government had launched proposals to make continued federal scholarship aid for students contingent upon draft registration, and protests quickly began to be organized. A group of faculty members had also signed petitions objecting to the continued presence on campus of the Hoover Institution, an independent but strongly affiliated center at Stanford that was credited with much of the analysis behind the policies of the Reagan administration and had supplied several of its senior staff members. The hostilities grew, eventually leading to the creation of a faculty committee and, later, a group of Trustees to review the Hoover/Stanford relationship. In subsequent years, this dispute was destined to mature into a longer-lived furor, involving a proposal, emanating from Hoover, to bring the Ronald Reagan Presidential Library to Stanford in a close relationship with that institution.

Significant controversy also arose over legislation in the Congress that would have outlawed mandatory retirement of university faculty members: Provost Al Hastorf and I publicly supported the retention of mandatory retirement, believing it essential to the tenure system and to continued faculty replenishment, but a few colleagues argued that the views of the entire community should be sought and reported, not just the administration's. That raised a deep, almost constitutional problem about the character of the University—a matter touched on earlier.

Sports often provide a relief for life's more trying moments. Alas, relief never came. A football season that had seen some inspiring moments, including an upset of the nation's then-number-one-ranked team marked by the heroics of quarterback John Elway, ended with a bizarre and galling defeat at the hands of our rivals from Berkeley. Their five-lateral kickoff return at the game's end provided a decade-long supply of video highlights, negated another great performance by Elway—and left more gloom in Palo Alto.

So there was something for everyone to be edgy about; and that winter it seemed never to stop raining—a circumstance we would, in later years, have welcomed joyously. Even the Stanford visit of Queen Elizabeth failed to stop the deluge. It didn't bring a halt to controversy, either: try as we would, we could not devise a guest list and a lottery that seemed fair to all claimants.

The deepest-lying issues of the year, however, turned out to involve the University's research programs. The problem of indirect cost recovery made its first appearance as a prominent source of difficulty in Stanford's relationship with the government. The long-standing policy of full recovery of the indirect as well as the project-related costs of doing government-sponsored research was put under serious threat, partly through Congressional inquiry but primarily through the action of the National

Institutes of Health, which proposed arbitrary limitations on recovery. That debate would continue, episodically, for another decade. And within Stanford there was a controversy that, although local, was even more intense. It involved the Stanford Synchrotron Radiation Laboratory, a facility utilizing the Stanford Linear Accelerator. A joint university-industry project, with collaboration also from the Lawrence Berkeley Laboratory, planned to build a new "beam line" to deploy high-energy synchrotron radiation for a variety of investigations. The project was fully supported by those faculty members who would use the new facility. But a number of students and staff, mostly at SLAC, were opposed on the grounds that some of the research activity would have military applications; they demanded that Stanford not build the facility. There were several petitions and two fairly well-attended marches on the President's Office. The real issue had to do with the freedom of faculty to pursue their own research programs, and eventually the Committee on Research saw it that way. In the meantime, I responded to the request that Stanford intervene.

"In the present instance, we have a research program that will produce some output clearly related to nuclear weapons testing. A careful reading of the proposals reveals that in fact a wide variety of work, including a number of programs on the fundamental properties of living materials, is to be conducted. . . . Sometimes the search for knowledge leads one to unexpected places; no research can safely be predicted to be free of harm— nor, conversely, can a piece of work that includes a military end-use automatically be defined as 'bad.'

"That is why the Committee on Research and the Senate reached the conclusion . . . that University restrictions on research would not be imposed based upon intent or end-use, but only upon conduct. The Stanford faculty decided that to open the door to prohibitions of this kind would, in the long run and in the aggregate, do more harm than good. It foresaw that today's benign restriction might become tomorrow's suffocation: that once you begin making value judgments about the possible outcomes of scientific work there is no place to stop. In summary, we placed our faith in the ultimate net benefit of free inquiry.

"I therefore do not plan to change the University's policy on research in order to eliminate the proposed program, nor do I think that my colleagues should wish to do so. I would hold that view even if the project under consideration were much more heavily devoted than it is to end-uses with which I am personally uncomfortable.

"Good general principles often get their severest and most meaningful tests in such uncomfortable situations. That is why those who are devoted to civil liberties sometimes find themselves defending dreadful people, and it is why the courts frequently have to release felons when it turns out that the police discovered their felonies in inappropriate ways.

"Our policy is that Stanford scientists are free to conduct work of their own choosing as long as it can be carried out in accordance with principles of openness and freedom of publication. The principle underlying the policy is that the social benefit flowing from free and unimpeded efforts to gain new knowledge will outweigh the cost exacted by the occasional pieces of dangerous knowledge we obtain as a result of free inquiry. Because I agree with the principle, I support the policy."

One of the most difficult things for a university president to do is to retain a serious connection with the scholarly discipline he or she has been forced to abandon as a central preoccupation. A few of my colleagues have managed to lead a semi-active research life while undertaking the presidency, but it is very hard to maintain anything like full engagement. The best one can do is to accept an occasional invitation to talk about it, and use that as an opportunity to think along once-familiar lines. At the University of Oregon convocation, I had a welcome opening to talk about post-Darwinian views of "human nature." The subject matter is one that has fascinated biologists and social scientists for years, and occupies the center of many an intense controversy: how much are we (and, most especially, our intelligence) influenced by "nature," that is, our genetic endowment, and how much by "nurture," that is, social influences? That issue pops up over and over again, always with surprising political force. It pops up in one of the incidents in this book, a dispute resulting from a speech by William Shockley, an electrical engineer who had developed strong views about the relation between race and intelligence. It reappeared in the contentious responses to the book by Herrnstein and Murray called *The Bell Curve*, in which the authors argued more strongly for the heritability of IQ difference than most biologists would.

"In addition to overthrowing the unity of natural philosophy, Darwin launched a new and troubling vision of humankind. The shaping of form and function—the 'nature' of organisms—by natural selection raised the prospect of a phylogenetically determined *human* 'nature.' That prospect, reinforced by twentieth-century genetics, has in turn reformulated some of the most profound social issues of our time. The Darwinian view of natural selection was promptly seized, and promptly misapplied, by proponents of the world's great systems of political economy. Herbert Spencer, and a succession of clumsier imitators like Andrew Carnegie, employed 'survival of the fittest' as a justification for the human competition in 'free enterprise.' In doing so they mistook economic fitness for reproductive fitness, an error occasionally repeated by foolish men and women even today.

"The Marxists, on the other hand, found the vision of biological determinism so deeply threatening that they were driven to extraordinary inventions for getting political economy back into the driver's seat. They were desperate enough to reach back a century before Darwin, to a failed doctrine that held inheritance to be under direct environmental control. The establishment of Lysenko's version of Lamarckianism as a state scientific religion in the Soviet Union for a third of the twentieth century was the result. Anyone who doubts the power of the connection between science and culture should examine that case as a cautionary illustration of its potential for mischief.

"Today one would suppose, listening to the largely political debates between Right and Left over how much to attribute to

Nature and how much to social forces, that the same issues are still dominant. Surely they found an acrid focus around the coined discipline of sociobiology. The key question claimed by the sociobiologists—how behaviors can be selected when they primarily influence the survival of others and not the behaving individual—is an important one. But it is hard to see it as the centerpiece of our understanding of cultural and biological co-evolution—let alone of how we should organize political economies! And the focus on sociobiology has overshadowed some more interesting cultural consequences of post-Darwinian thought.

"These, I would argue, involve our most basic notions about freedom, rationality, and equality. And the questions arise not out of genetics and evolutionary biology but out of the human sciences themselves: psychiatry, psychobiology, and neurobiology. In historic terms the real scientific successor to Darwin was Sigmund Freud. To Darwin's base of phylogenetic determinism, Freud added the mind as part of what was determined; and he also added a powerful set of ontogenetic determinants to the phylogenetic ones. Human nature, in the Freudian view, was dominated by evolutionary shaping and by 'early influences' on the psyche.

"In effect, Freud made the mind part of biology. Kant had recognized madness to be biological, but held all else in the mind to be moral and rational. Freud and the modern psychiatrists, biological and behavioral, put all mental process on the same continuum; they made mental illness part of the human condition or, perhaps, even the reverse. Alan Stone points out that '. . . psychiatry, after declaring madness a biological disorder, is haunted by biology in its understanding of the rest of humanity.' And he goes on to say: 'All of the dominant conceptual paradigms of modern psychiatry, biological and behavioral, conflict with traditional ideas about free moral agents.' One does not have to go that far to perceive the challenge that psychobiological determination poses for the notions of free will and moral obligation.

"Indeed, in just a hundred years, the biological sciences have triggered a most extraordinary reordering of our concept of what it means to be human and to be free. It is a view so new and so robust that it sometimes threatens to crowd out traditional choice and conventional morality. . . . The World shrinks as the Self swells. If there is a defect in our behavior, if we fail in what we suspect may have been an obligation, there are a host of comforting explanations: selfish genes, oppressive early experiences, or defects in catecholamine biochemistry. Finding an ethical path within our new vision of Self is one of the great tasks of contemporary humanism. . . .

"That brings us, finally, to equality—or rather, it brings us back, for it was the impact of biological determinism on notions of equality that tempted Carnegie and the Marxists into their futile wrestling-matches with evolution. Darwin's intellectual legacy is not merely that some individual differences are a consequence of biological endowment, nor even that these may involve the 'mind'; it is that these individual differences are substantial enough to react to subtle selective forces, and give rise to large differences in reproductive fitness. *The Origin of Species* and its twentieth-century offspring—genetics, psychiatry, neurobiology—have brought us to an expanded view of what is within us, as opposed to what is without. As a consequence we are obliged to enlarge our respect for the degree of individual difference.

"What does that say about equality? To many, it seems to damage the very notion. That view—held by many of those who are most repelled by the idea of biological determinism—seems to me quite wrong. Equal is not identical; different is not unequal. Social equality, that is, equality of opportunity, is simply not on the same continuum of choice with biological similarity. To admit a degree of inherent difference does not constrain our views on equality. It would be tragic if it did, for we need more and not less respect for individuality, which *means* difference. The great challenge for human society, it seems to me, is to abandon the denial of biological differences, and turn to the reformation of social opportunity so that it can fairly and gracefully accommodate those differences."

One of the liveliest and most accomplished groups of students at Stanford comprises about six hundred candidates for the MBA degree. These "Biz School" students take a demanding two-year course that at one time was considered barely respectable by the academic mainstream. But interest in and competition for the program has grown, along with the distinction of the Business School faculty. The Graduate School of Business is now annually ranked either first or second in the nation, and normally admits students only after they have taken excellent undergraduate records into the "real world" for several years.

The GSB students regularly sponsor major conferences, and do a superb job of organizing them. Sometimes their zeal and enthusiasm can be a little wearing, though, and occasionally they overlook larger issues in a way that makes one think they are learning only about "the bottom line." I had this feeling when they organized a conference on entrepreneurship that seemed to consider only the capacity of entrepreneurial zeal to generate profit.

"Entrepreneurship is one face of a great American tradition. Individualism, the capacity of a good idea to succeed, the vigor and vitality of independent activity—these are all qualities we hold in high esteem, and properly so. Much of our current economic vigor depends upon jobs created and technologies developed in the venture sector of this economy. To have a good idea, to get others to share some risks on its behalf, to stick to it until it's worth something, and then to persuade everyone else that it is—these things take a lot of personal courage and initiative. I suspect you all rate these qualities high on the list of virtues. I certainly do, and that is why I am glad to be here to salute your interest and your commitment.

"But there is another side to the American tradition, the complement to the entrepreneurial spirit; and while we all celebrate that one, I think it is a good idea that we remind ourselves of the other. This second side of the coin is obligation—public service. Not everyone is in the position to have a great commercial idea, or to benefit from the good ideas of others. Whether we like it or not, American society is not, probably never has been, a perfect market in which the benefits of entrepreneurship are distributed broadly and there are no external costs. (That is why it is not enough merely to do well by doing good.) It is especially important for those of you who are focused on that kind of success, and very likely to achieve it, to remember that you also have a more direct obligation to the society at large, and especially to those less fortunate than you, that is not discharged merely by the success of your ideas, or even by the tax revenue they generate. Ironically, the more successful those ideas are, the *more* what I have just said is true. So I hope you will think about the need to devote some of the personal energy and creativity you bring to the business of innovation to the public good in other ways as well."

That conference had occurred in late May, and the public service theme was very much on my mind as Commencement approached. The speaker was George Shultz, who had returned to government for the fourth time—leaving the Stanford Business School faculty and his campus house to become the second Secretary of State in the Reagan administration. Even the Democrats at Stanford who had found much to criticize about the Reagan presidency—and I was one of them—had enormous respect for George. He willingly returned to deliver the address at Commencement (and, it turned out, was equally generous with his time to students and others on his eventual return to campus at the end of the Reagan term). It is hard not to take advantage of the presence of someone who has occupied no less than four Cabinet-level positions by saying something about the importance of public service.

My opening text for this last lesson is supplied by the line from this year's Gaieties: "I think perhaps it's time I explained what's going on here."

What's going on is that you are in the very act of graduating from Stanford, and it is now my privilege to address you for the last time in your present status. So we have reached that point in these proceedings at which, by ancient custom, we examine together the timeless question: "Is There Life After Stanford?"

Since there are obviously alumni, there must be life after Stanford. I will say a few words about that in a moment. But first, there is something else: it is called the Awful Awakening. I refer to the realization that life off the Farm, although ripe for discovery, contains some problems. During the Awful Awakening, you will be envied and misunderstood. These are your crosses to bear. Perhaps they will be easier for you if I briefly acquaint you with each.

Envy, you must remember, is notable especially for its occasional irony. A typical example will help you identify it: Susie, a member of your high school class, was rejected by Dean Fred in the Spring of 1979, when you were accepted. Subsequently, you have learned (through the assiduous efforts of others who know you both, but know her better) that she was elected to Phi Beta Kappa at Princeton in her junior year, made all-Ivy in soccer, and has just been accepted to Stanford Law School. That's not the worst. Her mother—who is a good friend of your *mother— turns out to be your seatmate on a long transcontinental flight. As she settles in beside you, she begins the conversation: "Isn't it too bad that Susie is coming to Stanford just as you're leaving, dear. Do tell me about your plans." Misunderstanding can be even more immediately depressing than envy. Your Stanford penchant for abbreviation, so easily understood and accepted here, will only draw blank stares elsewhere; "Wide Libe" is not used in Cambridge. And only the Stanford interns in our Nation's capital will understand that by Mem George you mean the Washington Monument.*

You will, furthermore, have to accustom yourselves to a belief that this university resides in a middle-sized suburb of Fairfield County, Connecticut—or, perhaps worse, to a view that correctly places it in California but believes that it is in

*Southern California. You may recall that when you were fresh-
men my predecessor learned about the effect of distance on perspective the hard way, in the headlines: "New York Foundation
Post to Head of Coast School."*

*And finally, I would warn you sternly that you cannot expect
anyone to understand what it means when, in a difficult moment
of frustration at some injustice, you give the Stanford gesture for
confusion, personal ineptitude, and total loss of control. These
experiences of the Awful Awakening are unpleasant to different
degrees, but you will survive them, and once you have, you are
fully prepared to engage with Life After Stanford. In trying to
help you with this, I shall sound a bit avuncular, not to say
preachy. Too bad; that's an inevitable part of this ritual. It just
wouldn't be complete without farewell advice, so relax and try
to enjoy it. Last year, I approached my task by venturing some
hopes about what the graduates had obtained from their time at
Stanford. Here is a brief version of the list of qualities I gave
them: confidence in their own capacities of analysis; the desire
to appreciate and seek a wide range of diverse traditions and
values; a tolerance for ambiguity; a healthy suspicion of those
convictions that emerge from commitments to a single value; a
strong, but not incapacitating, skepticism about Certified Truth;
appreciation for the value of a sense of humor; and last, but not
least, a willingness not to be cool—to engage in headlong, risky
commitments when they seem warranted.*

*This year, I chose instead to make some predictions and sug-
gestions about what you may do with those capacities, beliefs,
and qualities that you will take away from Stanford.*

*The first is that you are likely to be soon occupied with a
number of matters you didn't study at all. This may produce, at
first, a sense of dismay. But I think you will then become ac-
quainted with an old piece of wisdom: that education is what
takes over when training gives out. You will find much scope,
even in unfamiliar circumstances, for the application of the capacity to communicate, the analytical style, and the foundations
of liberal learning that you have gotten here. I hope you will*

come to trust those capacities and believe in them. More than that, I hope you will tell others about your successes, especially those who have yet to begin college. They need relief from the awful burden of believing they have to Prepare for Life even before Declaring a Major!

Second, I urge you not to regard this day as the end of one phase of your life and the beginning of another, entirely different phase. Your years in the university should open doors but not close any; it is an episode of learning but it will not encompass all, or even most, of the learning you will do. If it has worked it will have expanded both your appetite and your capacity for more. Indeed, the only thing I don't like about the symbolism of Commencement is the metaphor it offers for the discontinuity between learning and life. I hope your life will be a symphony in some respects, but you won't, I assure you, live it in movements! Take from here the belief that the best that has happened to the life of your minds will happen over and over again—if only you will insist upon it.

There is a third hope, and I want to dwell on it at somewhat greater length. It is a wish that you will put some of the talent, energy, and training you possess into public service at some time in your lives. I offer that wish with the realization that these are not times in which that prospect has a great deal of natural appeal, even to an audience of thoughtful and compassionate people in the university that not so long ago led the nation in the rate of volunteering for the Peace Corps. We might begin, in fact, by wondering briefly how we could ever have reached a point at which public service requires such special pleading.

There is, of course, the state of the economy. Constriction of opportunity makes everyone more cautious about occupational risk-taking. While I take that seriously, I do not think it begins to provide the whole explanation. Other things have happened. For example, a decade's worth of unwise political rhetoric about Big Government and the Bureaucracy has congealed into a generalized mistrust of the public sector. Morale in federal agencies, about which I know a bit, has been sapped by constant criti-

cism—especially from those campaigning for national office in the hope that they might run those very agencies! Both the vulnerability and the resilience of morale in the civil service were poignantly illustrated by the way in which disheartenment at the Environmental Protection Agency turned to hope when the eleventh-hour restoration of trusted leadership offered those career employees the return of their self-respect.

Second, there are abundant illustrations of the cost of public service. For experienced men and women who have something valuable to contribute to their government, it is not easy to give up the comfort, the financial advantage, and the personal freedom that private life provides. No one, in short, needs to go into one of the visible, high-pressure government jobs; the reward has traditionally been a sense of fulfilled obligation and a measure of respect from one's fellow citizens—not immunity from criticism, mind you, but decent, humane respect. If that is allowed to disappear, we may some day wake up to discover that public life at the top has become such a psychic hazard that only the insensitive will undertake it.

A third source of difficulty, I am afraid, comes out of something that is actually rather good: our national rediscovery of entrepreneurship. It is a distillate of some traditional pieces of our national character: individualism, independence of action, innovation. Our economic situation, and our visible need for productivity improvement, have heightened the emphasis on private initiative and on new ventures. But passion for the entrepreneurial chase should not blind us to some fundamentals. We must take care of the agricultural and industrial basics. We must govern ourselves. We must teach the children. Despite what we are told by the best-selling Corporate Futurists, we cannot live in some Mandevillian beehive run entirely on smokeless information, in which half the inhabitants are venture capitalists and the other half software designers.

Entrepreneurship, we should remember, is but one side of the coin of American tradition. Obligation—public responsibility— is the other. The public sector has been through some difficult times, but its need for your support and your talents is only the greater because of that. Think of your own life, and consider how much poorer it would have been without the dedication of the best teacher you ever had, the most devoted leader in your community, the county agent, the city director of recreation—whatever public servants you have encountered in personally important ways. I find it quite inconceivable that you will decide, as a society, to allow those roles to be filled by whoever happens to fall into them. Yet unless we can manage to get some of you turned around, that is exactly what is going to happen. I am not naive enough to expect that any of you will change your life plan now; but I do hope that in the happiness of remembering this day, sometime in your future, what I have just said may contrive to touch your conscience gently.

Finally, I hope you will all find yourselves becoming advocates for what you have experienced here—becoming, that is, promoters and supporters of education at all levels. It is none too early for you to accept a remarkable fact: already our society's future depends upon those younger than yourselves. It is too late to do much about you; all I can do is stick a last word or two in your ear, and you're gone. But you can decide to use some of your own unusual educational background in the interest of improving the opportunities for those who will follow you. The quality of American education has never been more urgently in need of help from those in the best position to know how to help it—and they turn out, my friends, to be you.

Most especially, I hope that there will be joy and vigor and commitment in your lives, and happy memories of this place. Because I'm a firm believer in the sentimental marking of significant moments I close this farewell with the best testimonial to such remembrance I know of. It was said thirty years ago to another senior class by Adlai Stevenson, but it is independent of time or locale: "Your days are short here; this is the last of your springs. And now in the serenity and quiet of this lovely place, touch the depths of truth, feel the hem of Heaven. You will go away with old, good friends. And don't forget when you leave why you came."

CHAPTER FOUR

Looking Outward

1983–1984

Each fall the President of Stanford University participates in a rite that is, in its own way, as meaningful as Commencement. It is the other bookend in the academic calendar—the week during which we welcome a new class of incoming students. It is like the tidal cycle of respiration; we breathe out in the late Spring, and breathe in again in the Fall. The technical term, as well as the right metaphor, is inspiration. We get new, fresh air, ideas, problems, opportunities. And this inhalation raises once again our hopes and expectations for the extraordinary young people who come to Stanford.

We support the venture with a veritable outpouring of care, most of it organized by tradition by returning students themselves. Advising associates (upper-division undergraduates who serve as brokers and "extenders" in the freshman advising system), orientation volunteers (red-shirted returnees who meet planes, serve as greeters in residences, and the like), Resident Assistants (mostly seniors, who provide a more mature presence and serve as events coordinators and troubleshooters in the dorms in which they live) all return early to help with new student orientation. There are several hundred of them in any given year, and they give a spirited, warm introduction to the campus.

But despite such efforts, it is not an easy time for everyone. For the entering students, it is sometimes freighted heavily with apprehension. They somehow know that having been superbly successful in high school is no guarantee of more of the same. They inquire hesitantly about the accomplishments of their new dorm-mates, and often find them intimidating. Dean of Admissions Fred Hargadon liked to promise such students that in just a year their apprehensions will have turned to overweening confidence: the freshman who wonders how in the world he got here will become the sophomore who wonders how everybody else did.

Hard as it is for the first-years, it is sometimes even harder on their parents. The empty room at home, worries about their offspring's survival, the financial and emotional commitment parents make for their newly college-bound sons and daughters add up to abundant cause for concern combined with incipient sadness. If one has been a parent under these circumstances—and I had been one twice—it is not difficult to know the signs of separation anxiety. I evolved an approach that blended some humor with empathy, but also tried to give parents a hopeful parable to lean on in the bad moments.

"It's a great pleasure to be able to welcome all of you to Stanford, and tell you how delighted we are that you have been able to accompany your offspring here. We hope it will serve two purposes: to assist in their launching, and to convince you that someone in the family has made a brilliant decision. Indeed, I hope you are already arguing about who should get credit for it.

"And it is always amazing to me how such youthful people can possibly be the parents of college undergraduates. My own attitude about these proceedings, in fact, began to be shaken several years ago by the discovery of occasional former students of mine in the disguise of parents! And I am happy to report that earlier today, to their great delight, two different mothers have been asked about their room assignments. (The fathers are still hoping.)

"As one who has shared the experience you are now going through—once here, with an offspring who is (miraculously) a Stanford graduate, and once with her older sister who went elsewhere and is now even more miraculously practicing law—I wondered if I had any kind of wisdom that might make this occasion as comfortable as it is important. Perhaps I do. So let me deal briefly with two subjects that are likely to be at the top of your minds this morning: expectations (yours) and independence (theirs).

"First, regarding expectations. You already know that you have unusually capable offspring. You also know that you have something to do with their success, but not everything. We have a lot of difficulty in this country sorting out our feelings about the transfer of opportunity and of reward between the generations. We are pretty egalitarian, and we insist that it is merit that matters; what happens when a young person inherits too much, we say, is that they may wake up on third base at the age of, say, 26, and think they hit a triple. You have launched your young people with high expectations of what they can accomplish on their own.

"On the other hand, we *do* like success and are eager to reward it. As to that, we have access to the wisdom of Benjamin Franklin in a letter written to his daughter, Sarah Bache, in 1784, about the Cincinnate Society:

"'Among the Chinese, the most ancient, and from long experience the wisest of Nations, honour does not *descend*, but *ascends*. If a man from his Learning, his Wisdom, or his Valour, is promoted by the Emperor to the Rank of Mandarin, his Parents are immediately entitled to all the same Ceremonies of Respect from the People, that are established as due to the Mandarin himself; on the supposition that it must have been owing to the Education, Instruction, and good Example afforded him by his Parents, that he was rendered capable of serving the Publick.

"'This ascending Honour is therefore useful to the State, as it encourages Parents to give their children a good and virtuous Education. But the *descending* Honour to Posterity, who could have no Share in obtaining it, is not only groundless and absurd, but often hurtful to that Posterity, since it is apt to make them proud, disdaining to be employed in useful arts, and thence falling into Poverty, and all the *meannesses*, *servility*, and Wretchedness attending it; which is the present case with much of what is called the *Noblesse* in Europe.'

"So for what you have already accomplished you are prepared to become Chevaliers de Cincinnatus, and I congratulate you. Having thus disposed easily of expectations, I turn now to the more important and difficult matter of independence.

"On that subject I can offer you only limited comfort—and that is surely what you need—from beneath my hat as University President. Once upon a time I could have assured you that we would preserve and protect each tender aspect of your offspring's character, by offering zealous monitoring of their behavior and corrective guidance each time they were seen to stray. As you all must know, that is not now part of such an institution's role. We *do* try to offer support and help where needed, and I consider this to be, by and large, an affirmative and supportive place. We do not, however, engage in a lot of behavior modification. Instead, we try to display our attachment to certain values, and hope that the lesson takes.

"I may be of somewhat more help, however, in my role as occasional (and formerly regular) teacher of biology and student of animal behavior. There is a research result that I often recite on occasions like this; you may not find it encouraging at first, but from it I hope to develop a moral that may provide somewhat more comfort, if you can only engage in the willing suspension of disbelief for a while.

"We often misinterpret the development of organisms, and the role of external instruction in that process. That is because of the familiar tendency to confuse maturation with learning. In that regard, it is enlightening to consider the fledgling bird, who—popular lore insists—learns to fly by watching its parents. A more dramatic illustration of the need for parental supervision of the first forays into the world could hardly be found anywhere. Here is the fledgling, poised uncertainly on the branch; there the adults, chirping nervously and initiating short demonstration flights. Eventually, there is an imitative effort on the part of the young, amounting to little more than a semi-successful flutter, and finally there is perfection through repetition, accompanied by much of what can be interpreted as adult encouragement.

"It may or may not please you to learn that one biologist has done the experiment of raising fledglings in isolation from their nestmates and their parents. He even immobilized their wings by slipping paper tubes over them, so that they could not even perform the 'practice' gestures of flight. When their siblings out in the real world had successfully flown, the experimental birds were brought outside and the restraints released. They promptly took off and flew just as well as their supervised brothers and sisters!

"What is the lesson? I think it is this: at some point, the internal 'program' for further development is adequate, and unrolls without help. We are so used to the concept of external guidance of development that we mistake the process for one in which learning is taking place, whereas what we are really witnessing is the maturation of individual potential.

"It should not be necessary to say that people are a whole lot more complicated than birds. I would not suggest to you that the kinds of flights Stanford undergraduates will be taking here are made without the benefit of important influences of yours, and possibly even important influences of ours! But neither you nor we should underestimate the adequacy of the capacities they already bring to the challenge of independence.

"We are well aware of the importance of that. Indeed, we are realistic enough to understand that one of the crucial things we do is to gather—or, more properly, to *compose*—a freshman class with such a diverse array of talents, backgrounds, and potential for growth that their opportunities for mutual education are almost limitless. We and the other selective universities are thus fortunate enough to be able to perform a second valuable social function—namely, catalyzing the exchange of education among the young—in addition to the more usual function of supplying education ourselves. We need a certain humility to recognize that this catalytic function may, in the long run, be just as important as the other—no matter how highly we may regard ourselves as teachers and scholars.

"But neither function will work without a sense of adventure and an active seeking on the part of our students. Sometimes that can be painful: it means confronting hostile ideas, different orthodoxies, contrary assumptions. It may mean coming to grips with one's own limitations, and that is never much fun. But without it much of the potential of this experience will have been wasted. An enormous effort has gone into the composition of the freshman class of which you are now related parts. Its diversity has been guaranteed not only by a selection process that winnowed 17,000 applicants down to about 1,700; it also required a heavy investment of general funds in financial aid to guarantee the degree of social and economic diversity we are able to claim. But that effort and those resources will have been wasted unless your sons and daughters are persuaded that seeking out those differences and understanding them—and thereby coming to know a much larger part of this great American cultural keyboard—unless, as I say, they are persuaded that this is important and worthwhile, then much of the opportunity you and we have created will have been lost. In speaking to them, I have emphasized that this confrontation of differences is a rocky, often uncomfortable business, and that it will require of them much more than mere tolerance.

"I hope you agree. In my view, what we need to reinforce in the young people we care so much about is a sense of adventure, a willingness to take intellectual and social risks, and a curiosity about portions of the world that have previously been beyond their reach. For that voyage we can provide a good stock of opportunity, and eager hands to help. But we cannot compel, any more than you can, the drive to explore and to know. We can only believe in it, hope for it, and reward it."

That year my talk to the incoming class was unusual in one significant respect. The organizers of Freshman Orientation had scheduled a series of lectures to be given by Stanford Nobel prize-winners, of whom there were at that time about ten. Among those who had accepted invitations to speak was William Shockley, a retired professor of engineering who—in addition to the recognition he had appropriately received for his role in the invention of the transistor—was known for some controversial views about the relation between race and intelligence. When his presence on the program became known, minority students and others were outraged—understandably, because Professor Shockley's views really were quite extreme—and I was served with several demands that he be removed from the list of speakers. The issue had become very public indeed just at the time I was to welcome the new Freshmen, so I added an explanation:

"Tomorrow's program provides each of you a chance to learn through choice: to hear any one of the three scholars describe the work which led to the prize, whether or not you agree with his views.

"But that still leaves open more complex questions. Is brilliant scholarly accomplishment rendered less significant or valuable by later views, even foolish or reprehensible ones, in a totally different field? Should we deny ourselves exposure to the former on account of the latter?

"We would never face these questions as squarely or as forcefully were we not in a community that contains widely different views and backgrounds. These are real opportunities, even though they are sometimes painful.

"I suspect I need not remind you that freedom in our society has always been a fragile commodity. However, I feel a special urge to remind you that it's important for universities to cope with these challenges peacefully and successfully, because we can set an example for those parts of society in which freedom is sometimes not practiced so carefully."

Few national policies have been as meaningful for the great universities as those governing scientific research. A major theme at Stanford during the entire decade of the 1980s involved the relationship between universities and the federal government with respect to two issues: the national investment in basic research, and the need for government to leave the academic enterprise free to pursue its goals openly, without restrictions on publication.

In a speech to the Comstock Club of Sacramento in April of 1984, I had a chance to emphasize both themes in a setting that was suitably "political." Research policies are usually aimed at rather utilitarian objectives—particularly, improvement of the "science base," on which we are so dependent economically. As will become clearer later on, I gradually became more and more troubled by the degree to which academic research has been sold—indeed, has sold itself—on that basis, rather than on the values inherent in the educational outcomes it supports. None of these is more important than the goal of improving general scientific literacy, which I emphasized in the concluding portion of the talk. I began by referring to an issue that had become a huge national controversy while I was Commissioner of the Food and Drug Administration. A quack cancer remedy called Laetrile had gained prominence, and some groups of cancer sufferers—as well as politicians who strongly opposed regulation and favored "freedom of choice"—were demanding that the FDA's rules for new drug approval be set aside. A bill to legalize the stuff had over two hundred sponsors in the Congress, and a number of State legislators, including California's, had passed their own legalization statutes. It was a perfect case-history for looking at the problem of scientific literacy, and besides, I rather hoped that some of the California legislators who had voted for legalization might be listening, and experience some embarrassment. On reflection, I don't think either is likely!

"During my first year as Commissioner of the Food and Drug Administration, the nation was swept by the urgent belief that a substance called Laetrile, extracted from apricot pits and promoted by a phony Doctor of Philosophy, could cure cancer. This bizarre notion, for which there was not the slightest shred of proof, sent thousands of Americans off to seedy clinics in Mexico to procure it; produced a raging political controversy that led to extended hearings in both the House and Senate; led to statutes legalizing the stuff in nineteen state legislatures, including the one that sits in this town, and made the cover of *Newsweek*.

"A federal trial of the effectiveness of Laetrile was soon demanded, and eventually begun. But by the time it was finished, nobody cared any more. By that time they were all off worrying about the Scarsdale diet, or the psychic efficacy of pyramids. The scientific tests showed that Laetrile was without effect, the pseudoscientific rationale that had justified the treatment in the first place collapsed, and the fad was over.

"Now people merely joke about the souvenir ampule of FDA-seized Laetrile that I have in my office, and we've forgiven all those politicians who took this nonsense seriously enough to pass laws about it. I don't need to replicate this example for you: you can probably all think up your own. In case you cannot, perhaps it will suffice to remind you that the last poll taken on the subject revealed that fifty percent of Americans believe in astrology.

"What is going on here? I don't pretend to know, but I think it must have something to do with the increasingly obvious inadequacy of science teaching in our schools—related, perhaps, to a notion that seemed to take hold in the late sixties that it is good to have ideas and that all ideas are somehow entitled to equal merit. Whatever the cause, there are vast sectors of our society in which scientific literacy is alarmingly low, and in which respect for nonsense appears rampant.

"That gives us a general problem and also some specific ones. The general problem is that a nation without some system of scientific belief—that is, a nation in which astrology is taken as seriously as astronomy, and in which mysticism is accorded the same respect as rational analysis—is not likely to give sustained support to serious scientific inquiry. I welcome the heightened concern about the quality of our science and mathematics teaching in primary and secondary schools, and about the improvement of our public education system in general. Universities must recognize that they have an important stake, along with the rest of the society, in repairing the national lesion in scientific understanding. . . .

"American science deserves the respect of the American people—because it has earned it. If our society cannot bring itself to understand science—if instead it prefers fantasy and myth to data and evidence, and is the willing victim of charlatans—it will soon find that science is being done somewhere else, and that others are reaping its benefits."

The broader theme of education, its purposes, and its likely state in the twenty-first century, were the subject of the New York Alumni Conference later that spring. In it I returned to the matter of ambivalence about the purposes of higher education, and to the ongoing struggle between utilitarian objectives and the values inherent in the old term "liberal education."

"There is a continuing ambivalence in America between the utilitarian function of education and one more closely related to the traditional purposes of liberal learning. Let me now reflect on some of these more fundamental, traditional purposes of education at all levels. I hope for the healthy survival of each of the following four purposes, well into the twenty-first century and beyond. Education should generate a capacity to analyze and to communicate, not only adequately but, if possible, beautifully; engagement with a shared understanding of our heterogeneous culture and its multiple origins; an understanding of the natural world and its laws; and the ability to respect knowledge, and the process of acquiring knowledge, in a way that makes one not merely open to its lifelong pursuit, but insistent on that pursuit.

"These are the elements (not the only elements one could list, but surely major ones) of liberal learning. . . . These purposes should form the foreground of our society's expectations of education in the twenty-first century. If we yield too much to the utilitarian arguments, we shall find that we have produced the occupants of occupations, but not the citizens of a healthy State—people who can contribute to culture, who can manage their leisure time creatively, and who can be thoughtful participants in political affairs. We ought to ask ourselves not whether we are educating people to fill jobs, but whether we are educating them to carry forward the next steps in cultural evolution. There is, finally, a fifth entry on my list. I think that education should provide an understanding of the ways in which individuals act within their society—and of the principles that have been developed to shape and govern that interaction.

"That purpose is a little different, although like the others it is an important part of liberal education. Why is it different? It is because the special character of the schools makes it almost reflexive. The educational system itself is this society's great laboratory of shared responsibility—it is the place in which the individual first confronts the State, and it represents the State's most fundamental effort at discharging a collective responsibility.

"Thus the young person's very first day in school is a special kind of event—the maiden encounter between the private person and the public purpose. I think that students, even very young ones, sense this, and that it lends something to the mystery that leads almost every youngster to ask, at one time or another: 'What am I doing in school?' That may sound like a bad question, but as Mark Twain once said of the music of Wagner, it's not as bad as it sounds. In fact, it's a pretty good question. It probes a social mystery, perhaps the same one attacked by the youngster in the movie *E.T.* There is a moment in that film at which, having discovered the wonderful creature from outer space, the two brothers are headed off for school on their bicycles. The older one asks his sibling: 'Have you told him about school yet?' At this point the younger one says with evident frustration: 'How do you explain School to a Higher Intelligence?'

"'What am I doing in school?' The question seldom gets a thoughtful answer. You are here because of something called the

Social Contract—because of a set of old, deep-lying cultural arrangements that connect the individual to Obligation. It is a remarkable thing: the childless pay taxes for education, and they don't argue about it—because our culture believes in the diffusely distributed value of an educated citizenry.

"That particular lesson about being in school, which symbolizes and explains so much about the obligations we have toward one another in a well-functioning society, is poorly taught in the educational system at any level. The failure of children, and adolescents, and grown-ups, to understand school represents, I think, a defect in our capacity to understand shared social processes generally. A symptom of that failure is the low estate to which teaching and the other public service professions have fallen, and the low regard which many of our fellow citizens have for government. We ought to be ashamed when we turn out students who have not seriously examined the basis of their obligation to their fellow citizens—and disappointed if a significant proportion of them have not made a commitment to it by the time they leave universities like Stanford. This is surely a function of education that we cannot fail to repair before the twentieth century runs out on us.

"In short, we have far to go before we can guarantee the success of American education in the twenty-first century, and precious little time to begin the task. There are encouraging signs of the refreshment of political concern over the educational venture, and all of us hope for its sustenance and enlargement. What is needed is a change in the character of our national approach to human capital; a recognition that it is important; a realization that we have been moving our investment in the wrong direction, away from the critical early part of the life cycle; and a resolution to adopt tax and other policies that encourage a more appropriate pattern of investment. These changes, if they happen, may well come about in response mainly to utilitarian arguments: the enrichment of technology, the meeting of national productivity goals, and so forth. But there is an even more important reason for adopting them. It is the sustenance and continued improvement of our self-understanding and of our quality as a society. On that high road, education meets itself, for it is the primary instrument of a society's sense of its own emergent purpose, and of the evolution of culture itself. Its health, in Century Twenty-One, will be the best measure of the nation's health."

Commencement that year had outgrown Frost Amphitheater, whose capacity of about twelve thousand had forced us to limit the number of tickets we could allocate to each graduate. The welcome pressure of more and more extended families and more and more interest in the exercises forced us to seek a different venue. The idea of a Stadium commencement—adopted with great success in the ensuing year—met with heavy objections, so we tried Sunken Diamond. It was the hottest Commencement Day I could remember, and the setting was, for most, less than satisfactory. But a fine address by my predecessor, Dick Lyman, helped to rescue the occasion. In my own farewell I emphasized the matters that had been much on my mind that spring: the nature and future of education, and the meaning of obligation.

And now it is time, according to our ancient custom, to examine together the question: "Is There Life After Stanford?"

I begin by telling you that this is not my first Commencement of the year. I attended one as a parent three weeks ago, at a law school far from here. That occasion with my daughter Page reminded me of the depth of pride and satisfaction that families and loved ones experience on this occasion. I ask you again to think of yours—of the efforts made in your behalf, and of the love and the regard and the hope that fueled those efforts. They are not counting their sacrifices now, and they do not even need to be reminded of them. But you must find the words to tell them that their pride in you is understood, and that you are awake to the responsibilities it requires of you.

As I said in my introduction of President Lyman, this Commencement marks the end of a generational cycle. You seniors started in my freshman year, and from among you came my first

*crop of freshman advisees as president. I think it fitting to ac-
knowledge that passage by saluting Laura, Vaughan, Pat, Jane,
Bill, Jose, and Don, who have meant a lot to me and to Stanford
over the last four years. But what impresses me especially is
how well that small, random sample of the Class of 1984 mir-
rors the energy, the diversity, the talent and the potential of all
of you. It is, just as Dean Fred promised, a great class. In case
you're thinking that gets you home free, forget it. It merely
makes you worth all the excellent farewell advice I'm about to
give you. But before I give you the advice, let me restate a theme
with which I hope you are starting to get a little familiar. It has
to do with obligation.*

*You may be concluding that what's coming up is the speech
about The Privilege of Your College Experience, and what you
owe for it, so let's stop right there. Most of what has been happening to you here, I think, represents not what we have taught
you (though my faculty colleagues and I would be proud to stake
that claim) but the unfolding, under especially favorable circumstances, of capacities that you brought with you. Four years
ago, at the start of this voyage, I had a captive audience of your
parents in Mem Aud. After lulling them to sleep with a little biologist's parable about how birds really don't learn to fly,
which I will spare you, I argued that they should not underestimate what you brought to the process of higher learning. There
is a point, I said, at which internal programs for further development unroll without much help. But they do it better in the
right environments. We have provided a place—a rich, rewarding place. We have assembled a group of people who have much
to teach each other. And we have supplied good guides, and sig-
naled our belief in the life of the mind. But we should not fool
ourselves into believing that we have taught you what you have
learned here. You do have a splendid opportunity; but it is not
one we have given you as much as it is one you have earned for
yourselves.*

*Does that reduce your obligation? Not a bit. Obligations
aren't there because of what you have been given; they exist*

because of what you have to offer. You have the privilege and the duty to employ your opportunity in ways that are productive for the society you belong to. There is no Simple Perfect Way to the fulfillment of that obligation. Some of you may have been persuaded that public service represents a possible route, but there are others, and you will recognize them when they present themselves. It is important to keep asking yourself whether you are living up to the responsibility your opportunities have created for you—even if that involves nothing much more than performing superbly whatever tasks you set out to do. The reward is not merely the sense of fulfillment; it is nothing less than the infusion of meaning into one's life. John Gardner, Stanford '31, who is relentlessly quoted by admirers like me, put it better than I have ever heard it put in his talk at this Spring's conference called You Can Make A Difference. Here is what he said.

"In the stable periods of history, meaning was supplied in the context of a coherent community and traditionally prescribed patterns of culture. On being born into the society you were heir to a whole warehouse full of meanings. Today you can't count on any such patrimony. You have to build meaning into your life, and you build it through your commitments—whether to your religion, to an ethical order as you conceive it, to your life's work, to loved ones, to your fellow humans. People run around searching for identity, but it isn't handed out free any more—not in this transient, rootless, pluralistic society. Your identity is what you've committed yourself to."

That is not a bad thing to say to yourself, every once in a while, and then to ask how your sense of identity is doing.

Let us presume optimistically that you are launched on a path that recognizes opportunity and accepts obligation. What kind of use can you make of the things you have been given here?

First, I hope you will do some thinking about what education is, and what it is not. Wally Sterling said that it is what helps you entertain yourself, a friend, or an idea. There are also some things it is not. It is not, for example, training. I hope you won't find that out to your sorrow, but you may. Your education will prepare you for work in many important ways, but not primarily, experience tells us, by supplying specific knowledge that is germane to specific jobs. If you expect that, you are likely to be disappointed. And if that is all you expect, you are undervaluing your education.

Education is also no guarantee of anything. For a really full life it is quite possibly necessary, but it is not also sufficient. The formal version of this proposition we owe to the noted philosopher Casey Stengel, who said, "Say you're educated, and you can't throw strikes: then they don't leave you in too long." So education is not a free pass, but it is an essential beginning: a style of questioning, a way of going forward, an optical aid for examining life and then improving it.

Second, accept the world as it is, in all of its complexity, and have the patience and the courage to analyze and command that complexity rather than reducing it by simplification. Those who can boil every issue down to plain doctrine have a much easier time of it, but the fact is that we have a world overloaded with doctrine. That's because retreat to ideology is easy, and being righteous is so gratifying. But the great issues of life are too complicated to yield easily, and one of your obligations is not to approach them in a lazy way.

Third, don't fall victim to the social paralysis that results when we let visions of the best drive out the very good. Every program, every idea, every reform can be engineered a little more or made a little better by further massage. You have been encouraged to hold high standards, and that's good. But one of life's lessons is that you sometimes have to decide even when the data aren't as good as you would like. Similarly, you sometimes have to accept modest improvements rather than insisting on big ones. Remember that a lot of disappointed people have been waiting forever on the street corner for the bus marked "Perfection."

Next, at some time every one of you will have to decide whether to serve in some leadership role. I hope you will accept, even if it looks a little scary. The prospect of public failure and humiliation is daunting and full of risks, but the rewards are great. When you take up that challenge, remember that you cannot be universally loved in such positions, and that criticism, and even what I call ritual abuse, go with the job. If you're not getting any of that, consider the possibility that something may be wrong. If you are, test carefully to see if approximately equal amounts of it are coming from both political vectors. If so, you are probably in about the right place.

One warning: a possible overreaction to exposure is to become cautious about stating truths or beliefs. We will all be the poorer if candor becomes a casualty of public discourse because it risks too much hostility. On this point I am pleased to offer you further inspiration, this time from the useful forecourt player-philosopher of the Boston Celtics, Cedric Maxwell. He was asked by a reporter why he had broken the athlete's convention of off-court restraint by remarking that the Lakers had "choked" in game 4, and he replied with another great truth: "If you're that worried about the repercussions of honesty," said Cedric, "you should get a Doberman."

Finally, remember to touch bottom often. It is difficult to retain one's connection with the mainstream of our national experience when one has been educated at a great university, stamped by the certification into a leading profession, and then set down in a great metropolis. Yuppiedom does not conduce to a worldview, and neither does it conduce to a realistic view of the heart of America. The same, I hasten to add, might be said of permanent residence in an academic community like this one— but that's my problem and not yours. You may recall this point ten years from now when, in some elegant urban setting, you hear someone consult his long experience with Hyatt hotels and airport lobbies and claim that American culture has, after all, become regionally homogenized. Then it's time to haul out of there, to Berlin, New Hampshire; Newark, Delaware; Del Rio, Texas; Wisdom, Montana; Bend, Oregon; Sioux Center, Iowa; or Munising, Michigan. This is a great, splendid, diverse coun-

try. Its soul is not centered in the practice of law or medicine, nor in the pursuit of urban high culture, nor in a national spectrum of fads so broad that it comfortably encompasses nouvelle cuisine, break dancing, and Monday Night Football. Its soul resides, rather, in a clumsily defined set of values that blends a deep commitment to communities of manageable size with an equally deep respect for the dignity of the individual. If you lose touch with that, you better go back and find it.

That brings me, at last, to my usual last farewell greeting, given at another commencement, at another time, in another beautiful place by Adlai Stevenson: "Your days are short here; this is the last of your springs. And now in the serenity and quiet of this lovely place, touch the depths of truth, feel the hem of Heaven. You will go away with old, good friends. And don't forget when you leave why you came."

CHAPTER FIVE

Divisions

1984–1985

Stanford students who remember the academic year 1984–1985 would probably describe it as the year of the divestment demonstrations—although tension over that issue was to continue virtually unabated in the next academic year as well. Indeed, 1984–1985 saw a new peak of national and also local concern about apartheid in South Africa; few who shared that concern would have believed that in less than a decade a multiracial, democratic government would be established in that country.

There was little disagreement about the matter of apartheid itself, but a good deal about how Americans should respond to it. On the national political scene, the Congress was developing support for economic sanctions against the South African regime. A number of churches, universities, and other nonprofit organizations divested holdings in U.S. corporations that did business in South Africa—some selectively, some on an across-the-board basis. At Stanford many students and faculty members wished the university to take the latter course, and the issue produced deep divisions in the community. The Trustees and I held to the course of selective divestment. At one large public meeting I put the case in this way:

"It appears likely that if we can continue to employ the leverage represented by U.S. investment—and find improved ways of using that leverage—there is some chance that we can have a positive and long-term effect on conditions there.

"That chance, it seems to me, is the crucial answer to the argument that says: 'Divest—because we don't want to be involved with a regime that denies human rights.' In my judgment, following that direction might make us feel better for a short time, but then leave us facing the question: 'Did we really make a difference?' Because I think the results of divestment are likely to be no better than neutral, the act of divestment for me loses the moral force claimed by its advocates."

Strong feelings, however, are pretty resistant to argument. The divestment movement gained substantial force. At one point Joan Baez entertained a crowd of about 800 demonstrators outside my office on the Inner Quad; there were at least three major public meetings involving senior administrators, Trustees, and large audiences of students; and after one Board meeting a group of demonstrators blocked an array of Trustees' cars by lying down in the street, creating an unexpected windfall for Hertz.

The protests were significant in raising new investment policy issues for the University, and surely resulted in more serious use of the divestment prospect as a way of influencing corporate behavior. Stanford did divest its holdings in a number of companies that were reluctant to adopt the Sullivan Principles or to restrict sales to the South African government. But we declined to go down the road of wholesale divestment.

At times of great dispute on university campuses, one often hears students, faculty, and others raising questions about who "owns" the university. The question is posed as a challenge to whatever the normal mode of decision-making is, but it raises important issues regarding the origin and purpose of public trusts and the responsibility of trustees. Trusteeship and fiduciary responsibility entered the South Africa debate in a particularly direct form: if the advice of those who urged blanket divestiture were followed, and if it were to result in weaker performance by the University endowment, would that constitute a breach of "fiduciary duty"—that is, would trustees be liable for legal action on the grounds that they had violated the terms of the trust? That issue had been raised at several universities, and it became part of the debate at Stanford as well.

It happened that the year marked the one hundredth anniversary of the Enabling Act in the California Legislature that had made possible the Founding Grant to establish Stanford. The observance ushered in Stanford's Centennial celebration. The Centennial was described by one wag as the world's longest birthday party (it didn't end until 1991), but the anniversary that introduced it was not merely an excuse for an early start: it was an important legal milestone as well. The Enabling Act established the basis for public trusts in the state. On Founders' Day, I spoke of the trust and of the duties of trusteeship:

"The (California) legislature was persuaded that it is often desirable for private interests to be put at the disposal of public purposes, and ways have been found to create incentives for it and to protect its fruits. The very word 'trust' suggests the character of the approach: those who wish to make endowments for purposes that qualify as public benefits may rely on their restriction to the selected purpose. More than that, the arrangements envision, though they cannot guarantee, that the trust will be permanent. Fidelity to intention and the promise of immortality—those were the powerful incentives first offered to the endowers of public trusts. (Tax exemptions came later!)

"And these notions still form the core of fiduciary duty. When trustees conserve the purchasing power of the endowment by expending, in a given year, less than half the gain from that endowment; when they refuse gifts that would require an unacceptable deviation from the university's purposes; when they decline to commit their successors to a binding land use even when that use seems, at the time, highly desired by all—at these stubborn, grudging, recalcitrant moments, trustees are acting most like trustees and fulfilling their highest historic role.

"We as their agents are committed to the same duty. That document, a hundred years old today, reminds us that we are accountable to our own successors. In this creative, bustling beehive there are tens of thousands of voices clamoring for the present, as they should: more appointments, more fellowships, more relevance, more outdoor art, more responsiveness to the community, more construction safety, more victories, more . . . more . . . more. . . .

"In that clamor it is easy to forget the centennial message of that trust, which is that we must speak for the students who haven't been born yet, the faculty who haven't been appointed yet, the experiments that haven't been designed yet. From the past, the trust breathes reminders of Stanford's future.

"We are Stanford's custodians, not its owners; we and no one else can protect the centrality of its educational purpose and guarantee its accessibility to the next generation."

The events springing from the divestment movement produced a certain level of antagonism in a community normally devoted to more rational forms of discourse. So, too, did the proposal to bring the Ronald Reagan Library to campus—a proposal that amplified concerns of some faculty about the Stanford/Hoover relationship. Already, it was clear that the theme for much of my conversation with students would center on the difficult matter of disagreement without alienation.

A related issue was equally difficult, and equally important. To many of us, Political Correctness is both a phrase and a controversy of the nineties. But like most such phenomena, it surfaced much earlier than its highly public manifestations. Indeed, the novelty lies mostly in the term. The problem of Too Much Doctrine is an old one. Early in the fall, I spoke at the inauguration of Dennis O'Brien at the University of Rochester.

"The idea that only one kind of subject matter, or one kind of thinking, is correct is absolutely corrosive to our kind of institution, no matter what the political vector along which it arrives. The notion that history cannot be usefully interpreted from a perspective that lends more emphasis to the role of women is every bit as objectionable as the notion that some anthropologists can be ignored because they are 'biological determinists.' I never cease to be amazed at the vulnerability of otherwise creative and thoughtful parts of the academy to capture by doctrine. Whether it is the development of a policy center with subtle ideological tests for appointment or the establishment of rules that would regulate certain kinds of research on the basis of their prospective end-use, it is a perversion of the purposes of the university."

Such release to other academic venues happened rarely in the difficult year of 1984–1985. By late Spring, divestment demonstrations had become the most prominent events on campus, and the divisions on campus over this issue developed a harshness that prompted me to try and develop a Commencement emphasis on how to disagree without doing permanent damage. The weekend itself, as things turned out, did not provide an atmosphere that was very encouraging to that purpose. At Baccalaureate, former Dean of Memorial Church Davie Napier gave a bitter critique of U.S. policy in Latin America; and the speaker chosen for the major Commencement address, Governor Cuomo of New York, delivered a rather partisan political speech that turned out to be his eleventh graduation appearance of that year! In the aftermath, I got angry letters from parents and graduates alike, protesting that we had bathed our audience in a single set of political views. They had a point.

Nevertheless, it was important to talk about civility, and about preserving a sense of community even when the community contains—as it must in a healthy academic institution—widely divergent views about important matters.

And now it is time, according to our ancient custom, to examine together the question: "Is There Life After Stanford?"

I have begun my farewell to the graduates in that way each year, and perhaps because five years firmly root a tradition in this hospitable soil of ours, no one ever bothers to ask me what I mean. What I mean is this: will the vigor, the discovery, the sense of belief and hope, the depths of friendship, the sense of community—all of which I hope you have had in good measure during your time here—will those things continue to be a part of your lives? I pose the question because I so often encounter the persuasion that college, or education, is one thing, and subsequent life another.

How can we accept that? I believe that the period one spends in a university is a period of opening up, of conditioning receptiveness, of gathering comfort with self along with some wisdom. I believe it is the beginning of something, not the end, and I believe that it is an inseparable part of the rest of life. What you have from Stanford you will take with you, because it belongs to you, and in the end you will understand that it was not an episode in your life, but part of a continuous strand. I hope a few of you may remember the words from the end of Norman Maclean's great story: "Eventually all things merge into one, and a river runs through it."

But you will each bear some special marks from the Stanford part of your experience, and I want to talk about three of them. The first is the burden of excellence, and I have some advice for you on how to carry it lightly, and occasionally conceal it completely. The second is courage of conviction, and how to maintain it under pressure. The third and last, on which I want to spend the most time, is the capacity for disagreement without alienation.

First, the burden of excellence. One of the many entrepreneurs in this valley has made a nice little cottage industry out of T-shirts that say on the front "God, it's hard to be humble when you're from Stanford." But the shirt doesn't say anything on the back about how to deal with that problem. One of its aspects is real, the other imaginary. You were highly selected, and Stanford has probably also added something by way of value, though it's hard to tell how much. You may discover in yourselves a certain impatience with people who aren't as able, or as well prepared as you and your friends. That's the real part.

The imaginary part is wrapped around the expectations others will have of you: that you're very smart, or intellectually intolerant, or successful and quite possibly rich. Because that may make them edgy, my advice to you is to believe firmly in your own excellence, but keep it strictly to yourself. The only thing that will matter eventually, anyway, is accomplishment. Potential is all very nice, but if you are past forty and someone calls you "promising" you will abruptly realize that it may have been overrated.

Remember, too, that good performances are actually enhanced when they are accomplished in an understated way. Wisdom on that subject comes, as it often does at this time of year, from the playoff commentary of the Boston Celtics' forecourt philosopher, Cedric Maxwell, whose wisdom is valuable even in rare defeat. Of his colleague Dennis Johnson, who achieves effectiveness without dazzling advertisement, Maxwell noted that a number of players display their talent more noticeably. "But," he said, "D.J.'s here in the final, and they're home talking to their plants."

Next I want to talk about courage of conviction, a property much related to independence of mind. A good college experience ought to yield a powerful faith in one's own reason and analysis. I hope each of you has discovered the great, liberating truth that the tools of thinking actually work—that is, they yield the right result, even when used on unfamiliar materials in unknown territory. It is a fine thing to discover by these means that the textbook can be wrong, especially fine when the professor in the course wrote it. (You should be warned, however, that to question authority successfully is, in a way, to become authority.)

Even harder, I think, is to have enough confidence in one's own analysis so that it can survive the collective conviction of others. The power of conventional wisdom is enormous; so is the influence of peers. That power and that influence are reinforced by the comforts of consensus and of shared commitment. Only deep belief in the validity of one's own reason can keep one from being swept away. I am quite certain you have the power of reason, and I hope very much that you also have belief in it.

Most of all, I want to talk to you about a subject for which Commencement is not the most natural occasion. At such exercises we normally stress the themes of unity, community, and loyalty. That is only proper; we have these things in abundance, and I want you to remember them. It is a legendary belief of universities, after all, that nostalgia is a more appropriate mind-set for alumni than, say, critical reflection.

Nevertheless, I want to stress some opposite properties: diversity, individuality, and disagreement. Why? Because these are the important tests for us. It is not difficult to create communities of comfort. All you need look for is homogeneity among the participants, and a languid, accommodating style that permits like to settle in cozily with like.

At Stanford, we have made a different choice. We seek out and celebrate diversity—of background and experience, of economic circumstance, of special talents, and of ethnicity. We do that not only because it is right and fair, but also because it provides for all of us a chance to experience new qualities, new standards, and new convictions. Our heterogeneity yields richness. It is also full of opportunities for challenge, for misunderstanding, and for differences of view.

So disagreement there doubtless will be; the challenge is how to manage it gracefully. We have much to learn here about that subject, and one of the places that can teach us is the seat of our national government.

Now, a lot of things are done wrong in the city of Washington. It has a foolish affection for display, and it is insufficiently aware of what is going on in places like Palo Alto or even Albany, New York. But one thing they do understand in Washington is that the person with whom one is disagreeing today may be one's ally tomorrow, and that one should therefore take care not to scorch the earth. The ritual politeness that surrounds political contests thus has a function, and it is to be sure that re-

spect can be recovered afterward. The lesson is a valuable one: we have to have opponents, but we need not leave them enemies.

Now here are a few more notions about successful disagreement. It helps to grant to others the presumption of equal moral status. The more deeply embroiled in an issue one is, the more deeply one becomes convinced that one has the "right" position. It is easy to fall victim to the great optical illusion of moral superiority—the ground seems to be sloping away from you in all directions, even though it really isn't.

Next, we should resist the temptation to globalize our disagreements, whether over an entire person or an entire institution. I have a deep concern over this tendency, resulting mostly from my dismay at the increasing national habit of single-issue politics. The pernicious tendency to punish agencies, elected officials, or entire governments for actions or views on one narrow matter has led to a kind of paralysis of policy in this country. A senatorial candidate with a great talent for domestic affairs can be targeted for defeat because she is insufficiently pro-Israel; a congressman with wide foreign policy experience can be unseated because he has the "wrong position" on abortion. This attitude has become the despair of those who have better hopes for the American political system.

Let me assure you that single-issue politics has its manifestations in the University as well. Each year, I get letters from single-issue alumni (and even, occasionally, faculty, staff, and students) who forswear further assistance or loyalty to the University because of some dreadful thing it has done. It opposes the Baby Doe regulations, or it likes the wrong sculpture, or it supports the institution of tenure, or it lets the Band perform suggestive acts at half-time, or it permits experimentation on laboratory animals, or it has too little free speech or too much. Some of the complaints themselves may seem trivial. Others are desperately serious, and emerge from the deepest sort of personal conviction. All have a feature in common: somebody is prepared to invalidate the entire range of a great institution's activity as punishment for a single disappointment.

There are not very many great institutions in this world. Surely they deserve more than one chance each. And so do the people with whom you disagree. Each of them, too, is a complex landscape, with promontories of great worth and the occasional canyon of weakness. Each of them, too, deserves to be judged as a whole, and not discarded on the basis of a single feature. If we cannot restrict our disappointments in people to the part that disappoints us, we soon find ourselves rejecting more friends than we can afford to lose. Every such personal alienation is a casting-off of trust—indeed, of the capacity to love. By containing disagreement, that capacity can be conserved.

Differing with others is among the severest human challenges. As I said, it is easy to avoid it by seeking the comfort of homogeneity and of group-think. I hope you share my pride in the degree to which we have escaped that temptation. We are a diverse community; yet the comity of our time together in the University gives us hope that the learning and understanding and cooperation that have grown so well here can continue to grow well elsewhere. We have chosen a difficult path, stumbled occasionally, but covered a lot of ground.

So in closing, I want to thank you for all that each of you has meant to the life and work of Stanford. Your energy, your enthusiasm, and your concern for others has helped to make this a wonderful place to be. I hope you enrich other lives and other communities with these qualities, in just the way you have mine and Stanford's. And I want you to know that you go with my respect and my great affection.

That brings me to my usual farewell greeting, given at another Commencement, at another time, in another beautiful place, by the late Adlai Stevenson: "Your days are short here; this is the last of your springs. And now in the serenity and quiet of this lovely place, touch the depths of truth, feel the hem of Heaven. You will go away with old, good friends. And don't forget when you leave why you came."

CHAPTER SIX

Divestment and Obligation

1985–1986

It is impossible to review the events of 1985–1986 without reflecting on what a difficult year it really was.

The issue of South African investment returned unabated from the previous spring. By October there were demonstrations: a number of protesters were arrested after refusing to leave a sit-in at Old Union, and two days later a much larger occupation resulted in thirty-three arrests. One student, Robbie Perkins, charged that police had used excessive force in removing him and in processing him later at the county jail. As a result, Professor John Kaplan of the Law School was asked to undertake an investigation of the police misconduct charges. He found no evidence of improper conduct, but concluded that several procedures required improvement. Later there was a divestment march on the President's residence.

In Washington, tax reform was in full swing, and the universities found themselves on the defensive on a number of issues: the taxability of gifts of appreciated assets and the issuance of tax-free bonds among others. We lost on every one. Animal rights groups demonstrated against the use of animals in Stanford research, and mounted one "liberation" effort (unsuccessful) as well as a march on my office.

The Office of Management and Budget threatened to establish an arbitrary cap on university reimbursement for the indirect costs of research—an effort that was destined to have a dramatic and unpleasant echo in four years. Controversy was launched over Stanford's required curriculum in Western Culture. A visiting professor of history sued the University because he didn't get tenure. And so it went.

No issue was more persistently troubling, though, than the character of university finances—which had become prominent during the academic year 1985–1986. A stabilization in the growth rate of federal support for research, reductions in government financial aid for students, and a growing discomfort over the rate of rise in tuition costs all contributed to concern within the University. Outside it, however, the perception was that Stanford and the other "select" institutions were rich, and could deploy vast endowments for almost any worthy purpose. I began to give high priority to public explanations of the financial plight of universities—beginning with a talk to Los Angeles alumni on the subject of how we can look so rich, yet feel so poor.

"I want to tell you about an odd paradox, one that provides daily distress for those responsible for the welfare of the nation's major private universities. We find that balancing the budget each year has become a painful process of expenditure reduction, conducted amidst agony over the salaries we are able to pay our faculties and over the tuition we must charge. We see ourselves as lean, even stressed. But as we look outward, we find others asserting that 'we raise all we can, and spend all we raise'; that we have more endowment than we really need; and that we are not entitled to as much help as we now receive from private and public sources.

"Therein lies the paradox. At Stanford, in order to finance very modest levels of improvement in salaries and program quality, we have had to make moderate to severe cuts in our expense budgets thirteen out of the last sixteen years. That process has been a painful one, painful enough so that when we now ask for further reductions they are extremely difficult to find. Experienced observers, even those familiar with 'real-world' institutional economies, agree that there is very little fat left. So it is that as universities like Stanford measure themselves, there is a sense of being hard-pressed.

"Now, what I have just described adds up to a difficult situation. To look poor and feel rich in America is fine and honorable. To look rich and feel poor is no fun at all, and furthermore it is politically risky. What is going on here? Why do we find ourselves in this unenviable position?

"At one level, that question has a simple answer. Higher education is becoming more expensive than people would like it to be. That is because a good university education requires modern, high technology facilities and equipment and the services of creative, highly skilled professional people. In our economy, these costs have tended to inflate more rapidly than, say, consumer goods; thus the institutional 'inflation rate' at Stanford has usually run two or three points ahead of the Consumer Price Index or other goods-based estimates of inflation.

"But that unwelcome truth does not, by itself, explain the paradox. Two serious mismatches between perception and reality contribute much more to it. First, few people outside the universities are ever made aware of the real cost of education, because education is always offered at subsidized prices. Second, the public hears about university money in an unusual way: not in terms of annual expenditure requirements or annual income, but rather in the language of capital assets and fund balances. Yet those terms of reference would be quite out of place in the commercial sector. A billion-dollar company is not one that could scrape together a billion if it sold everything it had; it is a company that has a billion dollars in annual sales. The universities have the unique misfortune always to be labeled by their total assets.

"Now, these misunderstandings would be perfectly harmless if all they produced was an occasional gibe. Unfortunately, however, they have the capacity for much worse mischief. In what follows, I want to address the paradox of looking rich, yet feeling poor—in the hope that it may improve political receptivity to university needs.

"At almost every Stanford alumni gathering, people ask me why tuition has risen so drastically over the past two decades. Parents wonder even more poignantly, as do the majority of our students—who are on financial aid and find themselves balancing changes in their aid package against changes in tuition.

"It is helpful to differentiate between the cost of education and the price of education. At most first-rate universities, public or private, the cost of education is much higher than the price— that is, the tuition and fees actually charged to students. At public universities, the price is very much lower than the actual cost of education: the difference between cost and price is made up by a tax-derived subsidy that is given to all students, independent of their financial need.

"At a private university like Stanford, a variety of sources go to meet the cost of education. First, it is *priced* so that a significant contribution is made by the private funds of undergraduates and their families. The actual amount paid varies according to financial need: for poor students, the subsidy may be almost complete, whereas students with less need who pay nearly full tuition will meet more than half of the real cost of their education.

"In all, private funds derived from tuition payments by families account for about a third of the average cost of education for our undergraduates. The other two-thirds comes from a mixture of sources. The vast majority of undergraduate financial aid is derived from general funds, and is thus predominantly private in origin. A second component is represented by the difference between the full-tuition price of education and its real cost. That, again, is met mainly by private funds. The last fraction, direct government support from Federal grants and the Cal State Program, accounts for a very small fraction of financial aid; thus public funds are relatively minor participants in the real cost of educating our undergraduate students at private universities.

"Public universities, by contrast, set the price of education at a low value, sometimes zero for in-state students, and the large difference between that price and the real cost is made up by a mixture of state, federal, and some private funds.

"Thus the main difference between public and private universities is in the degree to which private funds participate in the meeting of public objectives. For the one-third of American students who receive their baccalaureate degrees from private institutions, the public investment is highly leveraged: in places like Stanford, each dollar of tax-derived money attracts three or four dollars in private support.

"In most public institutions the reverse is true: there is a relatively small private component—perhaps one dollar for every three or four public ones. Most striking of all, families with the capacity to contribute substantially to their children's education are not required to participate at all.

"That gets us back into the important matter of university tuition and the 'market.' The parents who ask why it is necessary for tuition to rise so far so fast are facing some harsh economic realities; but so is the university their son or daughter is attending. What are they?

"Over most income lines in our budget, we have very little immediate policy control. Our recovery of the indirect cost of research from the government depends upon pre-negotiated rates and upon research volume, and we can do little in the short run to change them. Income from endowment depends on a variety of external economic factors; we try to fund-raise actively—as our alumni know!—but results come slowly, not in the current year when we need it most. Tuition, then, is the only item over which we have significant immediate control.

"On the expense side, we have a budget 80 percent of which consists of salaries and benefits; there we are dominated by a need to keep able people in the face of external competition. Thus, like most salary-intensive 'service' industries, our inflation rate is two or three points higher than the Consumer Price Index. That requires us to move tuition ahead faster than the regularly reported inflation indicators for the economy as a whole. And that explains why sending a son or daughter to college has gotten more expensive a little faster, over the years, than a midsized automobile.

"That surprises a great many people with long memories; they often dissent vigorously, saying: 'It's a much tighter squeeze now.' That is true, and there are good reasons for it. The first is the remarkable change in *real income improvement*, over time, of men between the ages of 40 and 50. That is the decade in which most fathers are asked to help meet tuition bills. Between 1953 and 1963, the men in that decade improved by 36 percent in real income. Between 1963 and 1973, the ten-year gain for the equivalent cohort of men dropped to 25 percent. And in the decade that ended in 1983, there was actually a net loss of 14 percent for men between 40 and 50.

"Even families with constant or growing real incomes, find tuition payments harder to meet because they are forced to devote much larger proportions of that income to other things. A family living on the Peninsula sending a freshman off to join the class of 1964 probably spent less than 15 percent of income on housing. The price of a four-bedroom home in our area rose about eightfold during the succeeding 25 years, and rentals have experienced a parallel increase. It is not at all unusual now for families with college-age children to be spending 35 percent or even 40 percent of income on housing. To be sure, we are in an unusually expensive area; but I doubt if there is any part of the country in which housing costs have not doubled in proportional family expenditure since 1960. That has had a profound effect on family economics: not only does it tend to crowd out competing expenditures, like college tuition, but it has radically altered saving patterns, leaving families more poorly prepared to meet college expenses.

"Thus both the economy and the sociology of contemporary American life make tuition a harder stretch today than it was in 1960. It is, in short, not merely a perception that tuition payments are harder to make; it is a harsh reality.

"Why do universities have such appetites for growth? One answer is that by raising tuition about as fast as it has been increasing over the past decade, by improving salaries just enough to be competitive, and by fund-raising as we have been, we can manage a *constant program*—that is, finance last year's work at this year's prices, or do just about what we have been doing. Why shouldn't that be enough? Our student body, after all, is not increasing in size; and although there has been some modest growth in faculty, it is less than 1 percent per year. Yet each year our deans and department chairs present us with budget requests that, even after harsh pruning, add up to program increases in the vicinity of 2 percent to 3 percent. To leave room for that modest improvement, we have had to make cuts elsewhere.

"The explanation, I think, lies in the very nature of intellectual inquiry: behind our growth is an implacable law of the economics of knowledge. The great German physicist Max Planck was, as far as I know, the first to point out that new findings in science become increasingly difficult and expensive to obtain.

"After all, we tend to answer the easy questions first, and then proceed to the harder ones. Furthermore, we develop, in the course of our investigation, new methods and new tools to apply to subsequent work. So for a constant increment of gain at the research frontier, we find ourselves allocating more and more resources.

"Planck was speaking of the sciences, but it is the same in all the domains of inquiry. Just because we have invented computer science does not mean that we stop doing linguistics. On the contrary, we turn computers and the methodology of artificial intelligence to the problems of linguistics, making the latter at the same time more interesting and more expensive.

"I think that has much to do with life at the very edge of knowledge. To keep doing the same amount always takes more, just as Planck said; economic 'growth' is required to produce intellectual constancy. That is at the bottom of what we at Stanford have come to call the '2 percent problem'—that is, a per-

sistent unfulfilled appetite for improvement that really represents our bid to stay constantly productive.

"Our present portrait, to summarize it, depicts a group of institutions that look much wealthier than they are. They *look*
wealthy, and there is a related impression that tuition charges at
such institutions have risen much faster than they should, both in
terms of the capacity of families to pay and in terms of the real
needs of the institutions given the surrounding economy. Why
should that trouble us? It is, after all, not absolutely necessary to
be loved, or even understood. The universities are doing a good
job, they are generally well-respected institutions in American
life, and they can likely survive the misfortune of being thought
richer than they really are.

"The myth that the universities are rich and need no help is
not, by itself, so terrible. But when that myth contributes in its
own way to the pursuit of a short-sighted national strategy, one
in which we slight investment for the future in favor of solving
our problems *now*, it's troublesome. That approach will not only
damage Stanford and other universities; it will mortgage our national future as well."

The financial plight of universities was not the only educational problem on the front burner. The tragic plight of South
Africa and the responses of various American organizations
(from churches and other nonprofits to pension funds) were
making news. At Stanford debate was intensifying as the divestment movement, which its supporters preferred to call the
anti-apartheid movement, gained strength. The issue had been
left in a state of limbo at the end of the previous academic year,
with commencement demonstrations against Stanford's policy of
selective divestment. In mid-October, two occupations of the
Old Union resulted in about 40 arrests and the charge that Santa
Clara County and Stanford police had handled demonstrators too
roughly.

An appearance by Archbishop Desmond Tutu and more campus forums raised the tension, and in the late spring some two
hundred faculty members petitioned the Trustees for full dives-

titure. They were joined by Stanford's three senior Rhodes Scholars, and a group of some thirty former winners of the highest awards given at Commencement—the Dinkelspiel and Gores Awards. A culmination of sorts occurred when the Senior Class presented, as part of its class gift, a fund that was to be held in escrow until the University divested fully. At Class Day, I thanked the class for its gift, but could not avoid confronting the rather troubling principle it represented.

"Class Day is always a joyous occasion at which it is my own role to rise each year, as I do now, to receive the gift of the Senior Class. My pleasure on this occasion is as great as ever, but it is mixed with other, more complex feelings because of the particular character of this year's gift. So if in responding I strike a more reflective note, at somewhat greater length than usual, I hope you will understand.

"Part of what you of 1986 have given Stanford is fairly traditional; the other part is not. It takes serious intellectual wrestling to wrap a gift in a principle. The three Stanford Rhodes scholars, of whom I am very proud, thought hard about ways in which they could serve the University and still be true to their own convictions. Their idea of a South Africa-free-trust is, I would add, not one to which Stanford is hostile; indeed, various officers of the University have met with the trust's originators, responded to their requests for advice about its founding and management, and committed institutional support in every possible way. That is because we believe in individual choice, and because we respect thoughtfully reached conclusions even when we differ with them.

"But my respect and gratitude, abundant though both are, cannot change the central fact that this gift is not only wrapped in a principle but also has a string attached to it—one that provides an incentive for the University to follow a particular policy at the penalty of forgoing resources.

"To this student body, I suspect the string is seen as eminently reasonable. All of us, surely, share a sense of moral revulsion about apartheid. To many—perhaps most—divestment seems an appropriate and necessary signal of that moral stance. Others wonder whether disinvestment will really relieve apartheid, or doubt the links between divestment here and disinvestment there. But by now those arguments are surely familiar, and scarcely need rehearsal here. Suffice it to say that we have differed, and nearly always with mutual respect.

"What I would focus on now is not the rightness or wrongness of the conviction that led to the attachment of this string. Rather, I hope we might consider the appropriateness of employing our conviction on *any* single issue, however right or however widely shared, as a condition of support and loyalty. Surely there is no shortage of vitally important issues and causes, no dearth of particular principles that are capable of attracting passionate devotion from the majority at some given time. Will it be a good thing if, each in its turn, these others benefit from the precedent you will have established with this one? I wonder!

"I wonder how we will feel if, in the year 2020—my favorite target of retrospection, since you will be in charge and I will, I promise you, be a crotchety and cantankerous critic of everything you do—if, as I say, we find ourselves then walking together underneath the arches of the Inner Quad, looking at the lines of brass plaques (the successors to the one we laid this morning), something like this happens. 'Look here,' I tell you, rapping my cane on 1991. 'This trust has grown to four hundred thousand dollars. We get it the day the Medical Center frees all the laboratory animals. And here is 1996—nobody expected the Moral Majority to have achieved the impact it finally had by then! We get the '96 trust fund as soon as Cowell stops contraceptive counseling.' Well, I jest a little. The scenario could have been made a bit funnier, I hear you say; I answer that it could also have been made more plausible. We should never underestimate the capacity of issues to gain broad support, or our vulnerability to the temptation of making permanent our responses to them.

"Most of all, I hope we will not form the habit of judging complex, valuable institutions on the basis of their positions on a single matter. At last year's Commencement I worried about the globalization of disagreement, having in mind our increasingly pernicious national habit of single-issue politics. Governments deserve better; even more so, universities.

"Stanford exists for many purposes, all of which are related to the acquisition and dissemination of knowledge—the most precious commodity in humankind's relentless efforts at self-improvement everywhere, including South Africa. The University works toward those purposes in complex ways; its essence is that it is a web of process, with, of course, an appetite. To refuse to feed it because it is wrong in some particular dimension is, I think, to miss the point. We should ask ourselves about the fundamental rightness of its direction and the ultimate value of what it produces—not its capacity to be right every time, here and now, judged by a contemporary standard.

"Well, I don't want to be judged on my capacity to be right every time either. So I may be wrong in my suspicion that what we have here is a wondrously complex engine for social progress that we are somehow trying to improve by selectively punishing its carburetor.

"Despite that doubt, I am grateful to you for your generosity to your University, for your willingness to be thoughtful, and for your faithfulness to the tradition that in a great university the kind of dialogue you have stimulated—exactly this kind of dialogue—is what really matters."

That launched a Commencement weekend that might have been contentious. But it wasn't; there were some demonstrations, but the mood was anything but tense. The Commencement address was given by Ted Koppel, a Stanford graduate who has given his time generously to the University—and who would reappear four years later as master of ceremonies at the Centennial closing celebration. He dwelt on our impatient insistence on quick, simplified analysis and explanation, in the course of doing so inventing a great line: he referred to 30-second sound bites on television news as "McThoughts."

My own talk to the graduates was rather personal, and not at all directed at some of the year's more newsworthy institutional trials. I wanted to return to the theme of obligation, because it seemed to me that the trials themselves reminded us that we were all living in a time of unprecedented societal challenge.

And now, my friends, it is time for us to examine, according to our custom, the ageless question: "Is There Life After Stanford?"

The short but reassuring answer is "of course." There will be; but will it be what you expect? Well, that depends on what you expect; and that takes me right to my theme, which is all about expectations—the ones others have of you, and those you have of yourself.

To begin with, some people have had some very high expectations of you, or you wouldn't be here. That is a good thing: to believe the best about the capacities of others is probably the best way in the world to bring them out. Take inventory, for a moment, of the people who believed in you in that way: a parent, an older friend, a high-school teacher. Then resolve to let them know they made a difference.

I hope you have also found, here at Stanford, people unwilling to be satisfied with a low estimate of what you can do. Though our expectations are high, Stanford does not have the institutional habit of pushing them at people. I hope we've been patient when you needed time to back and fill, or to even waste some time and opportunity. But just the same, the expectations have been there, and we are proud of their fulfillment—as proud, in our own way, as the people who are sitting behind you. (So I would like to applaud you for a moment, and ask your families to join me.)

Now, the expectations of others sometimes have a way of being altered in translation, mysteriously converted from generalized belief and goodwill into prescriptions. They mutate into dicta about what paths a life should take, or what particular satisfactions one should insist upon. We all fight tense, silent struggles with these designs on the part of others. And when they are the designs of parents, we are put through trials of a special kind—trials that pit filial love and regard against what can sometimes seem like too much caring. In the end, fortunately, it usually works out all right for everybody. It is perfectly true that Charles Darwin's father wanted him to be a doctor—but don't forget, either, that later on he helped support his son as a naturalist.

Parents, though, are almost too obvious as targets for the charge of over-interfering expectation. Is Stanford innocent? I'm afraid not. Our expectations tend to be subtle, pervasive in the way an institutional culture is, and expressed in multiple images. You may remember this story: a freshman here for just two weeks came to Dean Fred Hargadon and said: "My roommate won the Westinghouse Science Talent Search, the woman across from me has published two short stories and a play, the freshman quarterback is three doors away, and down the hall is beautiful Wendy Wonka. Tell me, do you admit some of us just to be the audience?"

Starting at Freshman orientation and ending, maybe, in a few minutes, you've lived in an environment in which achievement matters, and in which excellence is celebrated. We attach great significance to the symbols of both. Yet I sometimes wonder, if, in doing so, we don't give more force than it deserves to the notion that distinction, in the sense of standing out visibly, is what success amounts to. Here are a few danger signals:

* *There is a focus on the "prestige" professions among Stanford students—a focus so intense that one advisee of mine some years ago, awash in a sea of premedical intentions, referred to herself as a "closet veterinarian."*

* *We have a program—Stanford-in-Government—that succeeds very well in attracting and guiding interns to the seat of federal government in Washington. But it has more difficulty*

generating interest in Sacramento, or in local government service.

• *Some of our alumni, hearing the praise we give to their most famous fellow graduates and listening to our continuous allusions to excellence, sometimes wonder whether Stanford is disappointed in them. They count their own contributions to community, to family, and to rewarding occupations—but wonder whether we are counting in the same number system. Are we placing too much weight on the glamorous and the distinctive, and failing to recognize deeper, more sustained—though perhaps more ordinary—forms of service?*

If so, we are surely inflicting thoughtless damage. Fulfillment ought to be available, without limitation, to all those who lead productive, considerate, examined lives. The really important expectations we have of you do not require you to be overachievers, nor to assume heroic proportions. The job description does not include leaping tall buildings with a single bound. Still, every single thing you do deserves the best you can give it. Much is made these days about why the United States isn't more competitive—why we can't be more productive and quality-conscious than other industrial nations. Well, the test in that competition is the capacity to apply ambition and intensity to ordinary work. If we can't get that done, we fail the test. In the end, even the most gifted and special people are judged by how well they perform on the things everyone must do.

So here are some revised expectations for you. First, we want you to be open systems and not closed ones, to seek continuing education and to welcome change. The most valuable thing about an education is the appetite it creates for more of the same. As this century races to a close, its most distinctive feature surely is the compression of the life cycle of nearly everything—buildings, institutions, and most particularly information. The useful life of a piece of knowledge is shrinking, and that makes change a compellingly certain part of your future. Stanford, by asking you to cope with newness, with unfamiliarity, with human differences, and with the dynamic state of knowledge, hopes to have convinced you that what you know matters a whole lot less than what you can learn. A corollary is that enough personal flexibility to welcome change is indispensable. I am here to tell you that it doesn't get any easier as you go along.

Second, we expect you to see a destiny for yourselves beyond your own immediate satisfactions. Surely you have expanded your view, in your time here, of how aching this world's needs really are. To have gone this far, to have seized the opportunity you now have, without resolving to devote some portion of your lives to addressing those needs would be simply unforgivable. And it would deprive no one more than yourselves, because—as you have probably come to know—few things are more deeply satisfying than to help make something valuable work better, or to relieve human distress.

As you search for opportunities, you might consider these candidates:

Item. Over 20,000 toxic waste dump sites have been identified, and 2,000 of them have been classified in the top priority list for cleanup by the Environmental Protection Agency. Only a few dozen have actually been worked on.

Item. We pay our teachers far less than we pay other professionals; worse, we treat them, not like doctors or lawyers, but like hourly wage-earners. When the schools don't do what we expect, we label it "A Crisis in the Teaching Profession." How ironic! If only we behaved as though teaching really were a profession, half the problems of the schools would be solved overnight!

Item. The candidates for 100 California State Legislative offices in 1984 spent $45 million dollars on trying to get elected, and they raised 90 percent of their funds outside the districts in which they ran—mostly from PACs and transfers. In that election, 98 out of the 100 winners were incumbents, perhaps because they outspent the challengers by 14:1.

That's just a little sample of ordinary, everyday, rotten things that need fixing. There are many more; many that may touch you more deeply than these. So the completion of this assignment, as they say, is left to the student.

Third, we expect you to be less risk-averse than we were! Nothing is so corrosive to the spirit, nothing so discouraging to the development of human potential as the fear of failure. And conversely, nothing is so liberating as the knowledge that failure and its most feared consequences are not so very dangerous to your health after all. That is the most reassuring single bit of experience I have to share with you; please believe it, because more than any other single attribute, controlling the fear of failure will allow you to control your destiny. So go for it.

Last but not least, I hope you can avoid the trap of generational chauvinism in which the United States is now struggling. In this regard, the example of my own cohort would be a poor one to follow. I am sorry to say that we have seriously under-invested in the intellectual capital of the successor generation, by diverting resources away from young Americans and by failing to maintain the health of those institutions—especially the schools and colleges—on which our national future depends. Most of you receiving Bachelor degrees will reach the age I am now in the year 2020. (Sorry, I recalculated it three times!) That would be a good time to apply some 20-20 hindsight to the problem: ask yourselves how you have treated the generation then graduating from college.

So much for our expectations. What about those you have of yourselves? In the end, that is what really matters, so the first thing I have to say about it is that your own standard, your own barometer, is more important than any of the expectations that others have been lavishing on you—even those who love you. You should listen to other people's hopes for you, but unless you have your own goals you'll always be working for the wrong people.

Having said that, here are three hopes for you anyhow; I was afraid you'd never ask. First, I hope you will set your standard higher than you can comfortably reach. Failure is not so bad, but low aspiration and easy satisfaction can be.

Next, I hope your future will include a heavy emphasis on sustaining each of your undertakings. At a time when superficiality is almost endemic to life, we need commitments that run deep.

And last, I hope that future will embody a special category for aiding the common good. That is as much in your interest as in the public's. Nothing is more thoroughly satisfying than turning one's own talent productively to the service of others, as so many of you have found out.

I hope you are prepared to make those commitments enthusiastically. As a caution—and, I hope, as a reminder of the importance of change—I want to tell you what you thought on your way in here, just four years ago. For better or for worse, you all made yourselves part of a record that the American Council on Education took down; it gives us access to your views before you came, and on how those views differed from those of your national cohort who were going elsewhere. So we have you on the record. Here are a few highlights.

You were more inclined than those headed for other highly selective private universities to consider it important to help others in difficulty and to promote racial understanding—but still, only 66 percent and 42 percent of you, respectively, listed these things among your "very important" goals. Only 29 percent of you thought you would make a change in your career choice, and only 11 percent thought that you would participate in a student protest. (You may be laughing about the second part right now, but just wait until you find out how wrong you were about the first!) Also, 58 percent of you thought "being very well off financially" was a very important objective, but only half that proportion thought that "participating in community action" was.

Do you see yourselves in that portrait now? What is different, and how? What made the difference—what friends, what experiences, what involvements? Or was it only your own maturation? Perhaps that will only become clear later. But surely you are changed, and just as surely you will change much, much more.

Remember that this is not the end, but merely the prelude to another beginning, one in which you just may recapture that freshman feeling, whether you want to or not. . . . In the immortal words of Yogi Berra, "it's déjà vu all over again."

That is the next to last thing I will say about expectations. The very last is about mine, for you: you are terrific, and my own admiration and regard and hope for you could not be greater. You have meant more than you know, to Stanford and to me, in your time here. I wish you a bold and fulfilling journey.

Now, I close as always with the Commencement admonition made at another beautiful place, at about the time of my own leave-taking from college, by the late Adlai Stevenson: "Your days are short here; this is the last of your springs. And now in the serenity and quiet of this lovely place, touch the depths of truth, feel the hem of Heaven. You will go away with old, good friends. And don't forget when you leave why you came."

The Dish Run was open to all comers, especially students, at 6:30 AM Tuesdays and Fridays. Sometimes they came, but not this particular morning. *Stanford News Service*.

An early Mark Wilson *Daily* cartoon, on the late-night fantasies of presidents. *Mark Wilson.*

Joan Baez entertains a group demonstrating for Stanford Out of South Africa on the Quad, 1985. *Stanford News Service.*

The 1987 Cardinal baseball team celebrates on its way to an historic championship in the College World Series—the first of two. *Stanford News Service*.

Part of Freshman Orientation included a bird-watching trip to the Baylands in 1987. *Stanford News Service*.

The Bass Center at Stanford in Washington is dedicated in 1988. *Left to right*: Robert Bass (now Chair of the Board of Trustees), Don Kennedy, Supreme Court Associate Justice Anthony Kennedy '58, Anne Bass. *Stanford News Service*.

Students demonstrate outside the President's office in the 1989 occupation over minority issues. *Stanford News Service*.

Trouble on the Hill: Chairman John Dingell of the House Subcommittee on Oversight and Investigations about to castigate Stanford for indirect cost accounting, March 1991. *Donald Kennedy*.

Tight End Cory Booker attempting a reverse Heimlich maneuver on the President, moments after John Hopkins' last-second field goal ensures Revenge for The Play. Big Game, 1990. *Donald Kennedy*.

The Last of Your Springs: Commencement, 1989. *Stanford News Service*.

CHAPTER SEVEN

Hard Choices

1986–1987

The academic year 1986–1987 was unusual in a number of ways. The difficult tensions over South Africa and divestment policy continued, and added to it was an unexpected national educational controversy over Stanford's efforts to make some rather modest revisions in the required course called Western Culture. These provided continuous competition with our efforts to launch the Centennial Campaign—the largest capital fundraising effort ever undertaken by a university.

In order to finalize plans for the Campaign and get it ready for the road, I took leave from regular presidential duties and established an office in Lou Henry Hoover House. There I tried an experiment in long-range planning with five young faculty and staff colleagues—which eventually yielded some institutional priorities for the post-Campaign period. I wrote text and laid plans for some of the Campaign events. And I took the opportunity, too, to find broader audiences for some views about the major national challenges to education.

During this time I became convinced that one of the central problems was a misguided attitude—leading to equally misguided policies—about social investment. A part of the argument was set out in a talk given to the Democratic Caucus of the

House of Representatives, at the annual Democratic Issues Conference.

"All human societies embody a drive to improve—to endow the successor generation with an enlarged and enriched culture, for transmission to *its* successors. Thus our own forebears liberated us from the 'short and brutish' life that was their own lot a few short generations ago; and thus our own obligation to our sons and daughters is to make possible a similar improvement for them. We undertake that task through a set of social arrangements we make to ensure the development of excellence in young people; how well we perform is the test—the ultimate, crucial test—of the *investing* society, that is, the society dedicated to its own future.

"At the center of those arrangements is the family—a deeply interested, important party, but never a fully sufficient one. Beyond the family lies an important set of proxies, as it were, through which we try to provide for the success of our children. Social welfare, public health, and—above all—education are part of that scheme. We no longer argue about the social justification for those investments. The childless pay school taxes as willingly as the parents, though it was not always so.

"At the apex of this system stand the nation's colleges and universities. They are of many kinds. Mine is one that happens to be fairly large, has a highly selective admissions policy, and takes responsibility for a lot of original research. It thus fulfills a mission that has been handed to a few dozen institutions in the country, one that has two simple parts: first, to train leadership for the successor generation; and second, to enrich the store of basic knowledge so as to power a cycle of improvement through innovation and extensions of culture.

"This task is simple to describe, if not to execute, and it has not changed significantly in half a century. Carrying it out is a privilege for me, one I accept with a kind of astonished gratitude. Among other things, it gives me a perch from which to view the most extraordinary young people in our country as they pass by. So I want to begin by evaluating the stock you and I hold in the successor generation, or—to put it in another way—I want to tell you about your sons and daughters. I use my own university as an example, but you may be sure that a similar description could be made of an institution near you.

"Stanford selected this year's freshman class of 1,500 from 17,000 applicants, of which 2,400 had perfect high school records. We look for promise, potential, and diversity, so we did not just select for grade-point perfection. Neither did we ask what they could pay; we asked only what they were worth. Thus our admissions process is need-blind; we accept the best, and then meet their full demonstrated need. And we ask them and their families to share a heavy investment burden with us. Sixty-five percent of them required financial aid in addition to those family resources, based on a tough means test. So in grant-in-aid alone, we gave our undergraduates $30 million, of which you people supplied only about $1.6 million. (Next year your share will shrink even further, if the Administration's proposed cut of 46 percent in the student financial aid budget is sustained.) Stanford is thus an agent for mobilizing private resources for the great *public* purpose of readying our best young people to undertake significant roles in the successor society.

"*Who* are they? They come from everywhere. A few are rich, some are middle-income, some are poor. Thirty percent are members of minority groups. From their diversity our students can gain a clear sense of the mixture of traditions, circumstances, and origins of this great culture of ours; and we hope they incorporate that experience into their classroom education.

"And *what* are they? Popular myth insists that they are self-absorbed 'careerists,' unconcerned with the plight of others. Nothing could be further from the truth. What they are is individuals, to whom personal scope and identity are important. Many of them dread being cast into roles in large, inflexible, impersonal organizations, or bureaucracies, a word we have taught them to fear. So they say they are 'entrepreneurial,' a word we have taught them to love. Their elders conclude from this that they want to make money, whereas what they really want is to make new ideas, make progress, make a difference. When we established a Public Service Center at Stanford three years ago to provide an outlet for these socially constructive impulses, our students swarmed to it like a starving multitude. It is the same elsewhere; an umbrella organization of such institutions called Campus Compact now has a membership of over 120 universities, and grows by the day. Peace Corps volunteering at Stanford has tripled in the past four years; a community outreach program enlists 800 volunteers for a full Saturday each quarter; today they are having an annual student conference called 'You Can Make a Difference,' this year devoted to families. In short, our young people are talented, they benefit from an historic extension of opportunity, and they have great enthusiasm for and commitment to their fellow citizens. Theirs is not the yuppie generation; ours is, because it is we who are delivering to *them* the debt associated with our consumption."

A hardy perennial in Stanford life—one to which we shall return in just a few years—is the chronic tension between the dual missions of teaching and research. That tension is exacerbated by the custom of calling Stanford and similar institutions "research universities," in recognition of a function they perform that others do not. It contributes to a notion that regularly appears at Stanford, that undergraduates get less attention than they deserve. As we began the Centennial, at the celebration of the anniversary of the laying of the cornerstone, I tried to deal with the question of balance.

"Within the Stanford family there is no more frequent misunderstanding, I am coming to believe, than the one we produce when we (and here I mean, most often, the current faculty and administration) use a particular term of art to describe Stanford and a few other institutions, private and public, with which it cooperates, competes, and often is compared. The term is *research university*.

"The misunderstanding, furthermore, is partly generational in character. Many alumni and alumnae from an earlier time have strong memories of this place that tend to be dominated by teachers and teaching. It is natural that they remember that and not the vigor and strength of the rather less conspicuous research programs that were under way then.

"But the term is also confusing within Stanford's present community. To our undergraduates it seems to take on literal meaning, to embody an institutional confession of priorities. It is seen not as it is employed in the language of higher education policy, as a way of differentiating those universities that have a commitment to knowledge production along with liberal education, from those whose commitment is to the latter alone, but rather as a claim of primary focus upon research. In that sense it bothers our students, who may see in it an invitation that draws their teachers into the library and the laboratory at their expense. The impression is worsened, of course, by the increasing difficulty in obtaining tenure for young faculty, here and elsewhere.

"So our undergraduates are worried that we don't have our objectives in order, just as some of you are worried. What are the sources of that worry? The first is a piece of folklore: that good researchers are likelier to be poor teachers than to be good ones. There is nothing new about that myth. It was prevalent here in 1960, when I first joined the Stanford faculty. It was not true then, and it is not true now. All of us have in mind, I suspect, a cartoon vision of the laboratory genius who mumbles incoherently through explanations of impossibly complex relationships while the class dozes. There are enough examples to give constant life to the myth, all right, but on the whole the truth is that people who are competent at one intellectual activity are likely to be competent at others as well. The list of past and present counterexamples at Stanford is legendary: Margery Bailey, Gordon Craig, Robert Hofstadter, Arturo Islas, Pat Jones, Eleanor Maccoby, Dan Okimoto, Colin Pittendrigh, Condoleezza Rice, Gordon Wright, Richard Zare; I could keep you here for quite a while.

"Another source is more complex, and it results from two trends. The first is one I mentioned earlier: tenure is simply harder to get, for reasons that have to do with demography and history. We grew rapidly in the 1950s and 1960s, and then tapered off dramatically as the economy moved into low gear. As a result the system is clogged with people my age, growing old ungracefully together. Then mandatory retirement was moved from 65 to 70, and soon it may be gone altogether. The consequence is a graying faculty, with far too few positions available for promising young additions. The second element is the increasingly demanding climate for research: fewer resources, more sophisticated and challenging technologies. I know of few Stanford professors who aren't having to spend more time than they used to in organizing, conducting, and funding their research programs.

"How do these elements combine? Clearly, they raise the incentive for faculty members to invest somewhat more, at the margin, in research. Of course our students notice that tension, and lament it—because they see choices made by their professors that disfavor them. And whenever, in this difficult climate, a favorite teacher fails to obtain tenure, it is cause for dismay— and for yet another contribution to our folklore that research matters and teaching doesn't.

"That is, in my view, a myth. I wish that undergraduates now could compare how much more seriously evaluations of teaching—including their own evaluations—are taken now than they were, say, twenty years ago when I was a department chairman preparing promotion papers. And I wish they could compare the quality and level of effort that goes into undergraduate teaching with what you remember from the old days, because I think it is very much the same. This is, as it always has been, a faculty that cares about undergraduates and about teaching. And so, despite the pressure to emphasize research, the day is stretched and the teaching gets done.

"But in the age-old battle between fact and folklore, folklore will win four out of five. Thus the recurrent student concern with our emphasis on teaching, and thus the winces that inevitably follow our references to the research university. And thus the urging, from all sorts of well-meaning colleagues, that I dispense with the use of the term—at least for the duration of the Centennial.

"I might be prepared to do that, but at least it deserves a decent, explanatory burial. So call this, if you want, a *requiescat in pace* for a phrase. Why did it come into being? What does it really signify about Stanford and universities like it? And in particular, does it really signal a dilemma for us—a conflict of commitment between the acquisition of new knowledge, on the one hand, and the processes of teaching and learning on the other?

"A remarkable postwar history of growth in academic science has led to the wonderfully intimate operational fusion of learning and doing that is the hallmark of literally hundreds of research settings that lie within a long fly ball of where we're standing. Here the line—and the conflict—between the acquisition and the dissemination of knowledge simply disappear. Its existence is in fact a very accurate fulfillment of the dreams Senator Stanford and David Starr Jordan had for the university they founded one hundred years ago. To California these two brought, from rural backgrounds in upstate New York, a set of strongly formed expectations about the work the new university was to perform, based upon a belief in the democracy of knowledge—a belief powerfully emergent in the late nineteenth century. Andrew Dickson White at Cornell had founded a university in which 'any person could find instruction in any study,' and in the public sector the Morrill Act had created a similar mission for the great land-grant universities. For Jordan especially, trained in the tradition of White at Cornell and of Louis Agassiz at his influential little biological station off Cape Cod, research was the heart not only of the university but of the educational process as well. 'A true university is not a collection of colleges . . . not a cluster of professional schools. It is an association of scholars,' Jordan told the graduating class of 1903, right here. In the same speech, he quoted his mentor: 'to know one thing well is, in Agassiz' words, "to have the backbone of culture."' Time and time again, he voiced his conviction that a professor to whom original investigation is unknown should have no place in a university. And he spoke admiringly of the German university, whose great function is—in his words—'instruction through investigation.' Perhaps the most compelling of Jordan's visions about education is his description of that process: 'The student begins his work on a narrow space at the outer rim of knowledge. It is his duty to carry the solid ground a little farther, to drive back, ever so little it may be, the darkness of ignorance and mystery.'

"These assertions seem modern to the point of banality, but at the turn of the century they were remarkable, and they described an education that in its time must have sounded revolutionary. It is a tribute to Jordan's determination, and Stanford's, that the description survived four discouraging decades and remained alive and ready to grow when the time was right.

"So this extraordinary fusion between learning and doing is alive and well today. And it is the outcome—as I have tried to show—not just of some fortuitous developments in American science policy, but also of firmly articulated and deeply held beliefs on which this university was founded. It represents now, as it did then, an important prospect for undergraduate education.

"Why prospect? The disappointing fact is that too few Stanford students are able to participate actively in this most special and rewarding kind of education. Their prospects are limited by insufficient opportunity, because the faculty is too thin to allow such mentorships to exist in the abundance we would like. Their prospects are limited by insufficient financial resources—to support research in the laboratory, the field, and the library, and to reduce dependency on earnings. Their prospects are limited by insufficient space, for our physical facilities, especially in the sciences, are increasingly inadequate for the uses to which they are being put. And their prospects are limited by their own choices—choices they might make differently if they were given more encouragement.

"A couple of years ago, Mortimer Adler cast a backward eye over a lifetime of teaching and declared that the so-called research universities could never match the quality of undergraduate education offered in the small liberal arts colleges. Their faculties, he argued, were simply too engaged with the tasks of research and with its rewards to spend the time necessary to do it well.

"I think that Adler is wrong, and that Jordan was right. The trick will be to take the extraordinary richness, the fusion between learning and doing, that universities like Stanford have—and couple it effectively to the upper-division experiences of undergraduates. The degree of difficulty is high: our faculty is stretched thin, we have our space limitations, and we have our other needs. But I am convinced that this is our most significant opportunity in commencing to build Stanford's second century. To it, we bring significant advantages: a faculty that is more diverse and more interesting than the one we would have appointed if teaching were our only mission; superb and ambitious students; and an array of exciting investigations that beckon for the attentions of both. So the Centennial Campaign effort is devoted to this proposition—the joining of learning and doing—more than to any other. If we succeed, it will amount to nothing less than a realization of Stanford's most significant founding vision."

The year 1986–1987 also saw the final steps of a difficult waltz with national politics. Stanford, in particular the Hoover Institution, had been chosen as the site for the Ronald Reagan Presidential Library. As has already been said, President Reagan's administration had made conspicuous use of Hoover work and of Hoover scholars, and this public affiliation had contributed to the tension between Hoover and a number of Stanford faculty members. Naturally, when the library plan was announced, there were objections. But two committees composed largely of Stanford faculty members—one appointed by the Senate of the Academic Council—had recommended that

Stanford accept the library. Most historians and other social scientists, including many who had ideological differences with the President, felt that the scholarly value of the resource should be the dominant consideration. The original proposal had envisioned, in addition to a library to house the Presidential papers, a policy center that was to be affiliated with the Hoover Institution. The Senate committee recommended, and I concurred, that the policy center be subject to the normal rules of academic governance prevailing in the University. We made this clear in discussions with the White House, in which the President was represented by Attorney General Edwin Meese. In turn, it was made clear to *us* that a policy center run by Stanford in the usual academic way would not be attractive to the President and to the Ronald Reagan Presidential Foundation.

Eventually, the Foundation announced that it would proceed with plans for the Library at Stanford, and pursue other options for the policy center. An architect developed plans for the Library on a site in the foothills, and a lease was executed. As the plans developed, architectural and regional planning concerns also began to surface. In many cases these were genuine; in others, one suspected that they were make-weights for objections that were in fact political. In any event, the plans were modified to meet many though not all of these concerns, and were eventually approved by the Board of Trustees.

But eleventh-hour concerns developed over some aspects of the design and—in particular—the visibility of part of the structure from Junipero Serra Boulevard and the back of the campus. The faculty Senate met to discuss a resolution asking the Board of Trustees to reconsider—not the invitation to locate the Library at Stanford, but these rather second-order features of the plan. The President of the Board of Trustees, Warren Christopher, and I were both present, and assured the Senate that although the Board would always listen to faculty views, the site and the plan had already been approved and would almost certainly be final. A rather mild resolution followed.

To our astonishment, the Ronald Reagan Presidential Foundation announced within a few days that it would make plans to locate the library elsewhere. It was, I think, a long-run loss for the University—though in truth the decision surely spared us a period of intense controversy. Sadly, it is still widely believed that Stanford "turned down the Reagan Library." Nothing could be farther from the truth. Despite some understandable misgivings, the Trustees and I made a proposal in good faith and delivered on every single commitment we made. Perhaps fear of controversy persuaded the Foundation to change its plans; perhaps some of the acrid public statements made by Hoover Director Glen Campbell during the negotiations persuaded the Foundation that it had a loose cannon on the deck. Some day, a careful history from an objective source will tell us.

Amidst the controversies over political papers, curriculum, and racial issues, some important accomplishments passed with relatively little notice. The opening of a lovely Stanford campus in Kyoto was a key event in the restructuring of the Overseas Studies program. We put in place a Program in Jewish Studies, which has since become a burgeoning, productive academic success. There was another banner athletic year, including four NCAA championships and a rare appearance by the football team in a major bowl game.

At Commencement, the main speaker was the Speaker of the House of Representatives, "Tip" O'Neill. A man familiar with change, he gave a talk full of his characteristic charm and humor. For my own part, it was natural, in a year so full of change, to talk about making choices.

And now, my friends, it is time for us to consider together— according to our custom—the ancient question: "Is There Life After Stanford?"

You know the answer: there has to be! I must tell you that you will never again be quite as free, in the sense of leaving room for exploration; quite as stimulating, in the sense of providing a group of peers who are bright and interesting and pointed in the same direction as you are; or quite as rewarding, in the sense of offering enthusiastic acceptance of what you are and applause for what you achieve. Whether you are finishing a doctorate or an econ major in the middle third of the class of '87, you have had an experience as devoid of arbitrary restraint, and as full of opportunity to innovate, as any you are likely to encounter later in life.

But I ask you not to let that discourage you about the future. Along with everything else—there will be more, much more, of everything good you have had here. My task, in these brief farewell remarks, is to suggest that what you have experienced at Stanford may usefully be applied to your future, to enhance its meaning and make it more exciting—to shape it, in effect, as an extension of what you have had here, and not as some entirely novel passage.

There are so many things that experience with an institution like this can provide, and I hope you have had all of them: the confidence that you can, as an individual, really make a difference in some outcome that is important to your society; the belief that you can confront novel problems, use your knowledge to suggest a solution, and then make the delighted discovery that it works; a conviction about the power of reason and the value of careful analysis; and—perhaps most important—a respect for the diversity of people and of institutions that makes you suspicious of easy aggregation, and pat solutions.

Each of these could be a topic in itself. But today I want to talk to you about something else that will be an important part of your life after Stanford. That topic is choices.

Now, you each will have to do hard things in your life and most of you have already had to do some. You will encounter situations in which your will is tested. You will be asked to live, at least for a time, with failure—failure that is all your own and can't be put someplace else. You will have to solve difficult problems, which is a challenge in itself, and then trust your future and that of others to the answers, which is an even harder test. You may have to endure disapproval and dislike, yet con-

trive to keep your self-respect. And you may even have to disappoint people you love.

All these challenges are hard; I know because I have had to face every one of them. But—at least in the formulation I have given—they appear as trials: objectives to be attained, consequences that must be endured. Choices are different—mainly because every time we make one, we have to give something up. That is true regardless of the character of the choice—and that is what makes choices difficult. Yet choosing is at the very core of human freedom and of responsibility as well. If it is true that education is preparation for the management of freedom and responsibility, then one of the things it ought to supply you with is the capacity to analyze choices, to make them with confidence, and to learn from the consequences while living with them. Surely Commencement ought to be a time at which one reflects on whether one's education has worked toward such purposes.

First, I ask you to think about choices that lie between desired things. Shouldn't such choices be easy? Experience suggests that they are anything but. The French have a wise phrase for an oversupply of pleasant alternatives: "embarras de richesses." Or, if you prefer contemporary American business argot, a choice between things you like is a "high-class worry."

Why in the world should it be an embarrassment or a worry to have two good opportunities? Simply because in making one choice we close the door on another. In the Frost poem:

> *Two roads diverged into a wood, and I—*
> *I took the one less traveled by . . .*

There is always a path not taken, and we don't really like to give things up. Choices like that are even the subject of an old rural New England joke, probably known to the Speaker as it must have been to Mr. Frost. The new hired hand is a miracle; he clears an acre of pasture in an afternoon, builds 200 yards of beautiful stone wall to edge it the next morning, milks the cows in ten minutes, and then is sent to the root cellar to sort potatoes. He manages to sort only three for the rest of the day.

"What's the matter, Silas?" asks the farmer; "I thought you were the hardest worker I'd ever seen." Silas replies: "It's these little decisions that kill you."

The economists, naturally, lay it out differently. They speak of the opportunity cost that is associated with any decision, including those that involve competing social goods. The attractive option one must reject is like the potato that might be sound enough; each is hard to give up.

However you put it, closing the door on prospects is a hard thing to do. That is why choices between attractive alternatives can be even more difficult, surprisingly, than the choices between good and evil, between appealing and distasteful. All of us love possibilities, and we feel impoverished when we have to give one up—even for a reward. Believe me, Silas the hired man is not alone. I have seen brilliant scientists so attracted by an hypothesis that they cannot bear to put it to their own cleverly devised test—because they know that the answer may reject a wonderful possibility. It is that reluctance, I think, that sometimes postpones our choices even when they seem terribly clear. How often have you deferred an obvious decision merely because you were reluctant to eliminate the glimmer of a possibility—even one you suspected was probably wrong for you?

I think the experience of an older chooser may be helpful to you here. It is important to recognize that the choices you have made are, after all, your choices, and that the paths not taken can be put behind you without leaving a plume of regret. They should be. That kind of nostalgia isn't good for your health; the world ahead of you is so full of opportunity you can't afford the time to regret what you didn't do in the world you leave behind you. The next line of the Frost poem suggests exactly the right stance; he follows the line about choosing the path "less traveled by" with this:

And that has made all the difference.

No regrets, and a solid conviction that the right choice was made—despite an evident lack of information, and with very lit-

tle to work with save a feeling that a little more risk, a little less familiarity, might be a good thing.

So much for the attractive choices—the ones in which each alternative is reasonably good, and the main danger is regret. What about the other kind—the ones in which we face a safe alternative that offers modest gains, and a risky one with higher rewards? Those can be very intimidating indeed; and a natural response is simply to defer the decision. By postponing such choices we are permitted to claim a kind of innocence, even pseudo-fairness: after all, we didn't actually damage anybody. Wrong. In just a couple of years in charge of a government regulatory agency, I had a lifetime exposure to the costs of non-decisions. There is nothing more corrosive, more discouraging to innovation, than the failure to choose in the arena of public policy. The costs fall everywhere, like a widespread drizzle, while we are permitted the illusion that it isn't really raining hard in any particular place. The very first head of the FDA, Harvey Wiley, put it well when he said: "not to decide is to decide." In fact, not to decide is the ultimate form of risk aversion.

That takes us, finally, to the most difficult personal choices we face—those challenges in which the contrast between risk and comfort is maximized. We have a powerful attachment to the familiar, to the place in which our confidence in friends and surroundings makes us feel safe and accepted. But if we opt for that comfort, we may shut ourselves off from the joy of accomplishment and venturing that is our reward when we confront difference and change.

It is exactly this issue that has taken some of our attention this spring. Stanford, I think, is well past the point at which it actively rejects differences in people, whether of political persuasion, ethnicity, race, or economic circumstance. We are polite, tolerant, even caring much of the time. But we still need to ask ourselves about the choices we are making. Are we actively seeking out difference, or welcoming new and sometimes hostile views?

I have had to ask that question of myself. The challenge that we have perpetuated forms of racism here is difficult to accept, for one who has devoted some personal effort to combat it. Indeed, the temptation is not to choose to come to grips with those charges, just as it is tempting not to confront the differences themselves. Far easier for me to "run on the record" of admissions statistics, or argue it out on the op-ed page, instead of hearing directly from those who are aggrieved. And far easier for you to stay with people who already agree with you, exchanging convictions that have already been rubbed smooth by familiarity, than to seek out discomfort and even confrontation.

Reaching out and courting risk is especially hard when one feels painfully unrewarded for it. We are used to receiving gratitude in return for such efforts. But in this world, that's an unreasonable expectation. Many of those on whose behalf we ought to be making uncomfortable choices, those to whom we should be reaching out, cannot be expected to react with grateful joy. They haven't been given enough choices of their own— enough to feel free, enough to trust. But even without the comfort of their thanks, we need to persevere in offering our own efforts. Things worth doing are worth doing the hard way.

So, to summarize, these choices are challenging because they invite us to relinquish security—through the sacrifice of comfort, or certainty, or both. Such sacrifices are difficult; but the ability to make them is the hallmark of the participating life. Oliver Wendell Holmes said it well: "As life is action and passion, it is required of a man that he should share the passion and action of his time at peril of being judged not to have lived." Were Holmes exposed to this time and place, he would have added another gender.

Most of all, I hope to persuade you that the life without choices is a life lived not for yourself, but for others. So I wish for you lives full of choices, followed by a minimum of regret. And I wish you lives rich in risk and discomfort, lived with a maximum of satisfaction. I hope your time at Stanford will have helped you make those hard choices confidently, knowing that you can master their outcome.

I will miss you, just as you will miss one another. So I send you on your way with some works of farewell and remembrance, said by Adlai Stevenson to another group of graduates in another place, but by now incorporated into our own tradition for this day: "Your days are short here; this is the last of your springs. And now in the serenity and quiet of this lovely place, touch the depths of truth, feel the hem of Heaven. You will go away with old, good friends. And don't forget when you leave why you came."

CHAPTER EIGHT

Culture Wars

1987–1988

The year opened briskly, perhaps even boisterously. At Stanford, as on many campuses, having fun had come to mean, all too often, drinking too much. I had brought this subject up in my talk to the incoming class, in the hope that more people would begin to take the issue seriously. Alas, the fall brought a minor rash of alcohol-related incidents, and the Interfraternity Council was persuaded to put together a meeting on the subject. Before a small and less than enraptured student audience, I tried to defend what I thought was a sensible middle ground.

"As all of you know, alcohol use is a problem, not just for this campus but for all campuses, and not just for young people but for all Americans. It shares with the use of tobacco the dubious status of being the nation's number one public health problem; each is so bad it's difficult to figure out which is worse, but in terms of morbidity at least, I think there's little doubt that alcohol wins—hands down, or possibly feet up.

"I became sufficiently troubled this fall to make this problem a central part of my address to the Freshman class, to the dismay of some who thought it was a bit of a downer. I said that I was distressed at the amount of binge drinking that goes on around here; I added that I thought studying hard five nights a week and then getting falling-down drunk the other two was not a good way to live a life.

"In a recent dorm appearance, I was asked what I thought an ideal alcohol policy was for Stanford. I answered that I thought we should proceed from a vision of what the ideal pattern of alcohol use was, and then try to decide what policies might be most effective in bringing that about.

"So let me begin there. I hope we might have a campus in which alcohol makes its appearance as an adjunct to, not as a centerpiece for, social functions. I would wish for its use to be secondary to other purposes, and moderate.

"Wherever alcoholic beverages have a link to regional or national cultures, traditions, or history, I would hope their moderate use might contribute to our understanding of those links; thus I see an intellectual element in the relationship of Puligny Montrachet to La Maison that I somehow find absent in that of Bud Light to the Beta House.

"In short, I recognize that alcohol consumption is a part of the pattern of contemporary social culture not only here but in most countries. I think a sound pattern of use would recognize that it can be consumed responsibly but not stigmatize those who prefer to avoid it entirely.

"Finally, I believe that the sensible, social use of alcohol can actually facilitate relationships, including those between students and faculty, so I would regret its unavailability for such purposes. The policies that will take us in that direction are, I think, primarily educational and not regulatory. Education consists of learning to make one's own choices, and that is why I think prohibition is of relatively lower value in our kind of environment.

"This is, alas, a difficult subject. I find it hard to talk about without sounding a bit preachy. And the mail I get is full of signs that people's lives have been touched by alcohol in ways so complex and disturbing that they find it difficult not to take extreme views on the subject. So the moderate route is, as usual, the difficult one to take. It is vulnerable to attack from those who cannot tolerate any incursion into individual freedom, on the one hand, and from those who cannot tolerate any deviation from enforced abstinence on the other. We shall continue to search for a middle ground, believing that a domain of responsible use exists, but conscious that it slides imperceptibly but swiftly into more dangerous terrain."

Through two generous gifts, we were able to open the Stanford campus in Washington, D.C.—a venture that has since fulfilled its promise many times over. Over 85 students a year now combine seminar and tutorial work with real-world internships in government and nongovernment organizations.

That was one aspect of yearlong theme of educational change. Stanford had a long tradition of leadership in thinking about the problems of schooling at all levels, and since the early 1980s—following the Study of Stanford and the Schools—had undertaken a more active involvement with local school districts. I had served on the Carnegie Forum on Education and the Economy, and one of its recommendations was for a stronger exercise of responsibility on the part of higher education for the K-12 segment. With David Hamburg, the president of the Carnegie Corporation of New York, and Russ Edgerton, president of the American Association of Higher Education, we gathered a group of college and university presidents at Spring Hill, Minnesota, to talk about how to fulfill that prospect. We worked out a consensus, which turned into an organization called the Presidents' Forum that has given the issue sustained attention.

The Spring Hill Statement, as it came to be called, tried to define a role for higher education in reforming K-12. In a talk before the Commonwealth Club later in the year, I tried to define a role for the federal government as well.

"Although I believe that the primary support and leadership for public primary and secondary education should originate locally, the problems are too deep-seated and too urgent to await resolution at that level. The school could be the hub for a comprehensive attack on the interlocked problems of at-risk children, and an imaginative deployment of federal funds could improve the schools while helping to rescue younger disadvantaged children. State-level as well as federal services are often Balkanized and hard to reach; the school is the logical place at which to integrate them. Preschool programs, interventions for poor children, education for high-risk mothers and older people might all best be headquartered in the schools, and incentive grants from the federal government to state or local agencies could provide a strong inducement to put them there.

"Teacher improvement is another critical objective that cries out for federal help. We cannot transform our educational system without powerful national leadership. It is one of the areas in which the President can, by speaking out knowledgeably and forcefully, change our attitudes and raise the morale of a profession in bad need of a lift. Hand-wringing about the poor quality of the schools and of teachers is not helpful; it is a form of blaming the victim, and we have had enough of it.

"A much more positive approach is offered by the report of the Carnegie Forum on Education and the Economy, entitled *A Nation Prepared*. Among its many useful recommendations is a program for certifying teachers as master or lead teachers. A Professional Standards Board has now been established to put that recommendation into motion, and former Governor Jim Hunt of North Carolina—who led a real educational revolution in his state—is in charge of it. Federal financing of a venture of this sort would be a significant initiative.

"Another area in which federal incentives have proven value is the improvement of math and science teaching. In the post-Sputnik era of the 1950s and early 1960s, there was a rash of curriculum-development activity that brought together scientists from the schools and the universities to study new ways of teaching and to share knowledge and technique. The changes in curriculum it produced were important, but not as important as the sense of professional continuity and elevated morale that was established among the K-12 teachers. That activity has been suspended for nearly two decades, but there is no reason it cannot be reestablished and extended—to cover all levels at which mathematics and science are taught in the public schools. The right vehicle is the National Science Foundation, which has the capacity to engage the science-rich institutions of the country in a way no other agency can.

"Incentive grants for encouraging the best and brightest students, especially minority students, to enter the teaching profession; teacher improvement funds that support in-service training or provide fellowship support for preparation in certain kinds of subject matter—these are other leveraged ways in which federal investment might improve schooling without interfering with more local policy leadership.

"There are, on the other hand, a few things likely to be suggested to the next administration that I hope it *won't* buy. One is a set of standardized national competency tests; another is a set of government definitions of what every educated person should know; still another is more commissions to study the problem and make further pronouncements about it. K through 12 education is regulated enough already; we do not require another set of tests that will persuade districts and schools to teach toward some nationally defined educational objective. As for defining the ideal curriculum or the perfect book list or the single page of questions everybody should be able to answer, who needs *that* from the next William Bennett or Lynn Cheney? Surely it is abilities and skills that will make the difference, not someone's notion about what facts and ideas we should all be able to produce on demand. And finally, haven't we had enough analysis of the problems in public education to know what will be required for reform? Will yet another hard-hitting critique of schools and teachers help, or are we just burning the village in order to save it?"

Back at Stanford, the theme of educational reform continued to echo, now expressed mainly through a sudden and intense debate over the revision of the Western Culture program. There hardly could have been a more prominent watershed in thinking through undergraduate education at Stanford. Changes in the required first-year curriculum to create a program re-titled Culture, Ideas, and Values placed us in the eye of a publicity hurricane, charged with the Death of Western Civilization. "Goodnight, Socrates" was the headline in one national magazine.

The matter first came before the faculty in the form of a report of the Committee on Undergraduate Studies, based on the work of a task force that had spent a year examining the curriculum. It drew immediate fire from some faculty critics and from the Secretary of Education, William Bennett, who charged Stanford with "dropping the West" from the program because of "intimidation" on the part of minority students. When formal discussion of the recommendation of the Committee on Undergraduate Studies began in the Senate on January 21, I introduced the discussion of the Committee's report in a way that I hoped was responsive both to the premature character of the internal criticism and the rather fanciful characterization of the Secretary.

"The subject we take up today is one segment of a large and complicated question: what ought to be the common intellectual property of every educated person? That question taps powerful convictions, and some of these have been at work already. They owe in part to our own cultural backgrounds and commitments, which in a diverse society are sometimes in conflict—often harsh but occasionally wry, as in Gandhi's probably apocryphal response to the question 'What do you think of Western civilization?' 'Worth trying,' Gandhi is said to have replied.

"Well, we are being asked what we think of Western Culture. Before we respond, I urge all of us, in this room and outside it, to remember that we are conducting a significant intellectual inquiry in a very public way. Colleagues whose likenesses are not regularly found in the *New York Times* are there this week. Significant outside persons—the Secretary of Education and Saul Bellow, to mention two whose views I once thought would span a rather broad range—have surfaced as commentators on what Stanford is doing even before Stanford is doing it. . . .

"I hope we can forget, as much as we can, these other audiences and concentrate upon our own objective—which is to help shape critical, committed citizens who will be prepared to exercise thoughtful leadership. What do we owe them? The answer, I suggest, will not be supplied by political denunciations of either stripe. Thus I think it unfortunate that the Secretary of Education has chosen to declare his view of an issue about which he is uninformed, on the basis of an outcome that is undetermined. It is surely reprehensible to assert that intimidation has occurred before the fact; but is it any better to seek to influence outcomes by turning harsh rhetorical judgments against those with whom one disagrees? That only makes it easier for those who wish, for their own political purposes, to demean this institution, its processes, and its judgments. . . .

"Spectators to the debate have done us a disservice. They have presented the issue as a contest between academic purists and know-nothings, between those who favor ultra-structured liberal education and those who believe there should be no structure at all. They have demonstrated that caricature comes easily in such matters, but we should not follow the bad example they have set.

"We should be clear that the recommendation we have before us is not a radical deletion of what we now have. Rather, it is a carefully drawn and thoughtfully reviewed proposal by colleagues who believe in a required core of studies as background to understanding our culture but who believe it should be somewhat broader than it now is. . . .

"Nor are its opponents zealous advocates of Eurocentrism; they are principled members of this faculty, many of whom have demonstrated extraordinary commitment to undergraduate education at Stanford. They differ honestly with the recommendation—to a degree about what we should do, but more about what we can do well.

"These positions are not polar extremes of educational philosophy, but different points along a continuum of fundamental consensus. Much too much has been made of the differences, and too little of their fundamental similarity."

The final debate took place in February, and was followed by still more controversy. Bennett charged in a speech at Stanford later that spring that the Stanford decision had been reached as a result of more "intimidation," this time by a crowd of students that had gathered outside the room in which the Senate debate had been conducted. He also reported a colorful incident in which the Reverend Jesse Jackson had led student demonstrators in chanting: "Hey, hey, ho, ho; Western Culture's got to go." In fact, Jackson had been on campus earlier that spring, in connection with his presidential campaign, and he had been with a group of minority students who employed that slogan. Several reporters on the scene, however, recorded that he not only did not take part in the chant but reproached the students, reminding them that they were of the West and had to learn about it.

In a debate with Bennett on the McNeill-Lehrer news program, I pointed out that the change to "Culture, Ideas, and Values"—the new name for the course—had left the West prominent, and that the intimidation charge was weightless. He was unconvinced, and I'm not sure either of us changed many minds in our audience.

The Commencement theme of challenge, and responding to challenge by maintaining one's faith under difficult circumstances, came naturally enough in a year when both natural and political forces had given Stanford all the challenge any institution could want.

Now I am allowed a few minutes for a farewell to my friends in the Class of 1988, and to those who are receiving advanced degrees. Ancient custom requires that at this point in the proceedings, we address together the timeless question: "Is There Life After Stanford?"

It is an opportunity I welcome. It provides a blessed relief from my yearlong preoccupation with the equally timeless question, "Is there too much life during Stanford?" And it permits me to reflect with you on the relationship between the experience you have just had and the life beyond it.

I make that distinction with some caution, because we have tried to make that relationship as seamless as we can. We do so by creating residential communities in which responsibility is shared and in which the life of the mind is encouraged to enter (at least occasionally). We do it by forming an environment that, in terms of human diversity, is unusually rich. We do it by trying to apply the extraordinary intellectual resources of this place to the abounding problems of the world outside. Our purpose is to make the experience of Stanford a part of larger reality—in some ways.

But in other ways we are, quite deliberately, an enclave where people from whom much is expected may try new things out one at a time instead of all at once. For people who are experiencing an array of new social and intellectual challenges, there is real need for a supportive and mostly cheerful environment. And, of course, there is the special character of academic villages: though more diverse in some ways than communities in the world outside, they are much more homogeneous in three important respects—age, intellectual potential, and purpose.

In our special enclave, we encounter many of what I will call the close-range problems of all communities. We have occasional disagreements about how we govern ourselves, the rules by which we ask one another to live, the basic respect and dignity we ought to offer one another as human beings. Intolerance, selfishness, racism—these we have to face, just as the rest of the world does. But we face them in a contained and unique system over which we are able to exert significant control. And we set very high standards for ourselves, so high that our failures sometimes distress us more deeply than perhaps they should.

For example, incidents toward the end of this spring quarter triggered a rash of self-doubt, and that in turn drew attention from the media—which, on this kind of issue in particular, are at least as effective at making news as they are at reporting it. There were undeniably bad consequences: members of some minority groups experienced pain, and to say that their pain is justified by the education that was its consequence is asking too much of them. But neither is it fair to charge us with lack of response, because this community showed a welcome capacity for self-healing. I doubt that at any time or place in the history of multicultural life in this country has there existed a much more powerful social conviction in favor of understanding and fairness than exists right here. That we often fail our own expectations says as much about our expectations as it does about the quality of our efforts to fulfill them.

I also believe that we have recorded some significant triumphs in the preservation of rational discourse about crucially important matters, ones that have sorely tested our capacity to disagree without alienation. In the debate over "Western Culture" this faculty and student body kept the real issues in view, even when outsiders were mischaracterizing them for their own purposes. In the compromise that was ultimately reached, everyone had something to be unhappy about (that's one definition of compromise!). But we realized that we had created something workable, and something better than we had before. There was a closing of the ranks—and eventually, I am glad to say, a gradual dawning, in much of the world beyond Campus Drive, of respect for our processes and understanding of what we had accomplished.

We have, then, a community that offers plenty of challenge, that performs well most of the time, and that—I assure you—you will miss in many ways. But its limited and special character shields one from some realities: not those of proximate communities, but those of the outside world with which our fates are entangled. It is easy to forget that our environmental destiny may be determined by deforestation 5,000 miles away; that poverty in a distant city diminishes us as it would in our own family; that we have as big a stake in arms control negotiations as those who are undertaking them. The Stanford enclave is an energetic and upbeat exception to the way things are working in most parts of the world, and you are about to find out just how much of an exception we are.

So for the next few minutes I want to talk to you about what you can do when you confront a discouraging world. The one you will enter is, of course, not all bad, but in some critical areas—population growth, poverty, environmental quality, international security—there is reason for deep concern. Indeed, at moments we all sense the uncomfortable possibility of Yeats's apocalyptic vision in "The Second Coming":

> *Turning and turning in the widening gyre*
> *The falcon cannot hear the falconer;*
> *Things fall apart; the centre cannot hold;*
> *Mere anarchy is loosed upon the world,*
> *The blood-dimmed tide is loosed, and everywhere*
> *The ceremony of innocence is drowned.*

The ceremony of innocence drowning is a troubling metaphor for your emergence from this splendid place. Yet you are well equipped to stay afloat, despite your drowning innocence; and I want to give you five suggestions that may be helpful.

First, please do go to work on the world's problems. They loom much larger when one cannot envision oneself as part of the solution. That is part of the philosophy behind the public service effort here, one that is even more applicable in the world beyond. An important corollary is that you will feel a lot better about the world's ills if you don't think you're adding to them. It is not for nothing that Hippocrates led off his string of aphorisms with "First do no harm." Evaluate what you do in terms of all its consequences, so that you have confidence in the worth of your commitments.

Second, don't become totally immersed. Leave time and room to change your focus; no one can spend full time in a vale of tears. The most conscientious have a tendency to feel guilty whenever they turn away from a serious problem for a bit of rest. Not only is that enervating and self-defeating; too much of it can make you boring, and a lot too much of it can make you a zealot.

Third, regularly gain support from those you respect and admire—and just as regularly give it back. Nothing overcomes discouragement, or renews energy, like praise. Indeed, considering the efficacy of praise in human motivation, it is just a marvel that there isn't more of it in the world.

Fourth, prepare for the future by believing in it. Franklin Roosevelt's theorem—"the only thing we have to fear is fear itself"—is confirmed over and over again by modern economists who understand that inflation, for example, is largely the outcome of aggregated personal fears about what may happen. If you believe, with some cynics, that "there are so many pessimists in the world because of all the optimists who owe them money," you really don't understand at all. Hang in there: the optimists are going to do better, and they will repay you with interest, late next week.

Last, believe that you can make a difference, because you can. Sustaining that belief is sometimes hard, especially when the world seems to be at the very bottom of Yeats's abyss—the point he reaches in the next two lines of "The Second Coming":

> *The best lack all conviction, while the worst*
> *Are full of passionate intensity.*

It is significant that Yeats finds the most discouraging element, the bottom of his vision, in the immobilization of good people. He is right. And remember that because of what you have been given by your families and by your society (including, I hope, this University), you are the best.

The restoration of conviction, when the best have lost it, often depends on choosing a corner of the problem and beginning to work on it, patiently and alone. Alan Paton, the South African author who spoke out steadfastly against apartheid when he was a lone voice in the wilderness, wrote a valedictory essay just before his death this past year that contained several quotations he had found important during his own life. The last one was

*taken from a stone tablet outside a country church in England:
"In the year 1652, when throughout England all things sacred
were either profaned or neglected, this church was built by Sir
Robert Shirley, whose special praise it is to have done the best
things in the worst times and to have hoped them in the most
calamitous." That, my friends, is a tribute worth having. And as
I bid you farewell today, it is with the wish that your best times,
as well as your best hopes, lie ahead of you.*

*There is one final thing to do, and that is to send you off with
a happy reminder of what this place has meant. For that purpose I employ again some words said at another commencement
by Adlai Stevenson more than 35 years ago; but surely as
meaningful, and as full of the right sentiment now: "Your days
are short here; this is the last of your springs. And now in the
serenity and quiet of this lovely place, touch the depths of truth,
feel the hem of Heaven. You will go away with old, good friends.
And don't forget when you leave why you came."*

CHAPTER NINE

Talking About Race

1988–1989

Few subjects are more trying, especially in a close-knit university community, than race relations. Even fewer are more controversial, most especially in a university community, than freedom of speech and any efforts to limit it. Race and speech emerged as dominant themes in this last academic year of the 1980s.

As the first-year class got its orientation, though, there were reasons to concentrate on other matters. Stanford had, I thought, put a little too much emphasis on community and not quite enough on academic purposes. In a Centennial piece on the university, a writer from the *New York Times* had taken a view of the undergraduate student body that I thought only a little unfair. Like many Easterners, he had found the atmosphere here academically rigorous but less "intellectual" than that at Harvard and Yale. I pointed out that there was an entirely welcome concern here with human relationships, and that it sometimes seemed to stress the personal rather than the theoretical. But I also worried that the custom of seeming cool and "in charge" of their academic lives might lead Stanford students to be less comfortable than they should be about bringing academic matters to the dinner table. (One thoughtful observer of the scene at Stanford likened our undergraduates to ducks on a pond who seemed to move effortlessly from place to place but were paddling frantically beneath the surface.) At any rate, I thought it was time to bring up to the entering class the issue of this odd habit.

"In its most harmless form, it consists of seeming more academically relaxed than one really is, keeping one's library habit in the closet. To get good grades but seem not to study is an admired bit of fraud around here, but you shouldn't let them fool you. The people who get A's and tell you they spent Dead Week in Hawaii have probably been studying under a sunlamp. In its slightly more virulent form, this countersignal entails feigned disinterest in 'serious' or 'heavy' discourse at mealtime; it is, I suppose, playing intellectual possum. And at its very worst, this attitude seriously discourages commitment to the life of the mind, by holding up to ridicule those who put that first and by repudiating their efforts to engage others.

"A specimen of this tendency was unwittingly delivered to my colleague Tom Wasow (then Dean of Undergraduate Studies) when he was being interviewed by a campus journalist about a newly established Dean's award for academic excellence. The reporter asked him: 'How do you answer the charge that this effort is an attempt to make Stanford more intellectual?' He was so bewildered that all he could say was: 'Charge?' Charge, indeed.

"I suggested to Tom that his first response should have been 'Guilty, of course.' Let there be no doubt that although community, character, and just plain fun are important around here, the central purposes of this university all pertain to the human intellect: its improvement, its expansion, and its application to the great challenges that plague our society."

As if in response to this theme, an event occurred that seemed monumentally unimportant to me, but somehow seemed to grip the attention of almost everyone else. The weekly newsmagazine *U.S. News and World Report* had begun, several years earlier, to rank the undergraduate programs of leading colleges and universities. Stanford had been ranked first or second frequently over this period, but in the issue that hit the newsstands early in October we slipped to sixth place. The drop was billed locally as a minor disaster, although no one stopped to look at why it happened: the magazine, instead of relying on the perceptions of academic leaders from around the country, had introduced a new ranking system that contained such "quantitative" measures as endowment per student and percentage of alumni giving. Fortunately, I had said publicly that such ratings were nonsense when we led them, and I felt comfortable in saying that the changes—which have continued—had made them no less nonsensical. The purpose of these ratings is to sell magazines, and one can only assume that they must accomplish it, since *U. S. News* has continued and even extended them—without, however, arriving at a method that establishes realistic categories or generates fair comparisons within them. Institutions as diverse as CalTech and the University of Michigan were being ranked in the same category. From the beginning, nearly all leaders in higher education have recognized the flaws in these beauty contests, and begged for their discontinuation—a movement that has now become quite active. Alas, relief is not likely to happen: prospective students and their parents appear to love them and, sadly, may even pay serious attention to them.

An event of much deeper local significance happened soon afterward. In Ujamaa, a dormitory devoted to African-American themes (but containing a minority of ethnic African-Americans), two inebriated freshmen, following a hallway argument, defaced a poster on the door of a black student's room in a way that was deeply insulting to many in the residence. It was an incident of a kind that has become familiar: an insensitive or ignorant person or persons perpetrates an offense against a minority group; there are calls for an institutional response to heal genuine damage; but freedom-of-expression issues quickly enter on the other side. Once again, Stanford found itself in the vanguard of a rapidly developing national issue.

As it unfolded I met repeatedly with students in Ujamaa and elsewhere, and decided that the healing process ought to begin well before the matter of sanctions against the offenders took us onto more complex and difficult terrain. I had a number of conversations with groups of minority students, and in an effort to start some serious discussions about the issue I wrote this statement on racial understanding.

"In a meeting at Ujamaa on October 17, I was urged by several students to write a 'thoughtful paper' on the issues raised by racial incidents here and in other campus communities. I am glad to comply, in the interest of setting out my own views and encouraging a more thorough discussion of these matters at Stanford.

"There is, of course, more than a hint of presumption in following up on an invitation to be 'thoughtful.' It can be a daunting temptation to failure, like the instruction 'be funny.' Moreover, the theme itself is so difficult, and so subject to divergent perceptions depending on one's own background and cultural perspective, that no discussion of it is likely to strike everyone as thoughtful.

"Nevertheless there are some clear objectives to begin with. What do we seek at Stanford? A pretty good summary, I think, would be this: a residential academic community of young men and women who are committed to serious intellectual purposes, and who are engaged actively in self-realization and in the support of one another. Our educational mission is achieved partly through a student residential community in which intellectual development is enhanced by practical experiences that help form views about what human societies are like, how they came to be, and how they can be improved. That, at least, is the hope. In the process of making residential life work, various visions are offered and adopted, or cast away; the relationships formed and the discussions undertaken in this context share importance with the curriculum. That is one reason we devote substantial resources to representing in our student body the full spectrum of ethnic, cultural, regional, and economic diversity that characterizes contemporary American society.

"In creating that community we have undertaken a formidable task. We are asking young people to ignore the habits of comfort, and to seek out others with whom they are unfamiliar and sometimes ill at ease. We are exposing them and ourselves to the risk of misunderstanding and even, when sensitivities are violated as they occasionally will be, hostility. But we think it is nevertheless worth the risk, because we are among the few places in this country in which it may be possible to test the workability of the multicultural existence that will, ready or not, be the life of Californians and eventually all Americans in the twenty-first century. To that pathfinding task we at Stanford bring a number of advantages: the choice to be here has been voluntary, there is an abundance of intelligence and goodwill, and we are engaged in a common enterprise that goes well beyond merely living together. If, with all these advantages, we cannot form a successful multicultural society, then it is hard to be very optimistic that one can be built without them.

"Yet even with them, the degree of difficulty is great—as we have been discovering. And our occasional failures raise important questions for us. How can we better prepare Stanford students to live with sensitivity and understanding in such communities? What is the role and responsibility of the institution, of its faculty, and of the residential communities themselves? How do we manage our occasional but inevitable disappointments, and guarantee that we can persevere despite them? The following reflections are not an effort to establish policy or even to guide in its development. Instead, I hope they may illuminate some of these questions, and thus help us to launch a discussion about our opportunities here and about our obligations to one another.

"At the outset, we need to be clear about our objective with respect to relations among the races. Is it to permit a casual separatism to exist, in which there is tolerance but only minimal interaction? Is it to encourage fuller integration? Do we value the retention of identity, or do we aim instead toward homogenization? These goals are often expressed in polar form, as though they were choices without intermediates. I believe, to the contrary, that we can retain the values of ethnic identity and, at the same time, promote a vigorous interplay among the various minority cultures and the (transiently!) majority culture. To insist either on full enclave status for ethnic theme houses, or that minority students be dispersed at random, will not achieve that balance. Creative experimentation with intermediates is, in my judgment, more promising.

"If Stanford continues along that course, we shall find ourselves experimenting even more with environments that demand a good deal by way of understanding human differences. They will continue to raise some of the questions I alluded to earlier, so I repeat them in different words. How can we strengthen the capacity of our community to encourage exploration and to treat matters of race in a sensitive and understanding way? How can we learn the vocabularies and the behavior of mutual respect? And how can we prepare ourselves to deal with the difficulties and discouragements that will inevitably arise?

"Because we are an educational institution and because it makes sense to begin with what you do best, we can make cultural differences an important part of what we teach. What I have in mind is rather different from the changes recently made in the design of the requirement in Culture, Ideas, and Values, and different also from the requirement in Non-Western Culture. We need to make the contributions and the experiences of ethnic and religious minorities part of a whole variety of courses that deal, in one way or another, with contemporary society. Perhaps the effort can be concentrated first on a few courses with large enrollments, but eventually it should reach across the curriculum. Dean of Undergraduate Studies Tom Wasow and his colleagues are now giving consideration to the kinds of course development that will be required.

"The success of that model, of course, will depend in part on whether we succeed in other areas. An extension of our efforts to teach about the contributions and experiences of minorities surely will require more minority faculty and other teaching staff than we now have. Their recruitment, already a high priority at Stanford, will never be as successful as we hope unless we, along with other institutions like us, can improve the availability of minority doctoral candidates for the academic disciplines. Various programs, including several supported by the recent grant from the Irvine Foundation, are now aimed at that objective.

"And of course there are other activities in this community that regularly afford opportunities for building understanding. Commitment to cultural activities, or the performing arts, or journalism, or athletics throws us into relationships in which common objectives submerge and often conquer differences that in other settings may divide us. Wherever powerful purpose dominates process, human interactions tend to go better. So activities from Ram's Head to varsity soccer, from the *Daily* to the Stanford Symphony, offer recurrent and refreshing examples of multicultural success.

"In all these aspects of our existence—academic, extracurricular, residential—our success has bred high expectations. Wherever disappointment follows, the reaction is painful, often bordering on grief. So we need to ask ourselves hard questions about our own vulnerability. Can the prospects of curricular enrichment, better management of our collective lives outside the classroom, all the other things we have talked about—can these remedies offer us immunity to incidents like the one at Ujamaa?

"I think we should not expect too much. Curricular change can broaden and deepen our understanding of difference, and of the ways in which diversity has historically invigorated our society. It can certainly remove areas of ignorance that now promote misunderstanding. But it cannot fully protect this community, or any other, from occasional expressions of insensitivity or downright intolerance. 'Ignorance is no excuse' became a well-worn phrase in the aftermath of the Ujamaa incident. That statement is true, yet unhelpful: some ignorance will survive even the best efforts at education, and it will escape in troublesome form whether we excuse it or not. Moreover, we are an open community that is characterized by rapid change, poor institutional memory, and a willingness to embrace new members at a moment's notice. It follows that some of us will always be unacquainted with the values shared by most people at Stanford. That should not discourage us.

"It is worth emphasizing, in this connection, that we are dealing with a broad array of challenges and not just with affronts to the black community. Here and elsewhere, there have been counterreactions against whites which, however understandable they may be, nonetheless represent a form of racism themselves. There has been a disturbing increase in the number of anti-Semitic expressions at universities, Stanford included. If we are to be consistent we must hold all such forms of expression to be equally unacceptable.

"But what does it mean, exactly, to say that some form of expression is unacceptable? If what we mean is that most members of the community will deplore it, that leaders will speak out against it, and that those responsible will be urged to change, that is one thing. It is quite another once we begin to talk about sanctions: dismissal or suspension from the university, loss of the residential privilege, or whatever. Withdrawal of membership in the community is a penalty that requires due process and a carefully worked-out balancing between the community's need for tolerance and good order and the individual's right to free expression. Freedom of speech is a powerful tradition in our society, and nowhere does it have greater or more special power than in universities, where unconventional and heterodox ideas are the very breath of life. I had thought that was well understood here, so I was surprised by how many members of the community were prepared to urge the swift and arbitrary application of sanctions in the Ujamaa case. Even now, there has been too little attention to the counterpoised value of free expression.

"Because we cannot hope that education is the answer for everything in this open and dynamic community, because intolerance and insensitivity can take so many forms, and because other values so often intervene in the treatment of racial matters, it is essential that we prepare ourselves to endure occasional failure without losing confidence.

"I have two observations to make about that. First, we need to remember that the best will in the world doesn't solve all the problems. I have observed a tendency here to search quickly, in the aftermath of each disappointment, for a place to affix blame. More often than not, it is 'the institution,' whatever that means; and the administration is frequently asked to provide the remedy. But Stanford is many people and many entities: freshmen, sophomores, juniors, seniors, graduate students; a faculty; deans of schools and of student affairs; workers; resident fellows and RA's; administrative staff; and so on. Some remedies are to be sought in one place, some in another. Some, perhaps the majority, are really the responsibility of the subcommunity in which the offense took place. Beyond the question of *where* remedial action lies, I find a little too much self-blame in our reactions, and I hope we can keep it under control. To take (or assign) realistic responsibility makes sense. To encourage a cult of culpability does not; it merely makes people who need to be part of the solution feel like part of the problem. We have accomplished much at Stanford, and we ought to be proud of that. When we experience reversals we should grit our teeth and move ahead, without elaborate mortification.

"Second, we need to acknowledge the feelings of hurt and anger that are often the result of bigotry or insensitivity. In the immediate aftermath of the Ujamaa incidents, residents told me that they frequently encountered the reaction 'Why were you guys so upset over that? Was it really such a big deal?'

"This problem is a very important one, and although it is the result of a racial incident, its solution has little to do with race or cultural understanding and everything to do with sensitivity and human understanding. It does no good at all to ask people who are hurt to justify their feelings; it amounts to telling them they aren't entitled to those feelings, instead of according them recognition and respect. The healing process begins with acknowledgment, and the offer of help that is the first instinct of friendship. In my orientation talk to the freshmen this year, I tried to make the point that we may have gotten so absorbed with diversity that we have forgotten our common humanity. It is still true that the safest ground for the exploration of difference is that common bond of family.

"Now I want to describe two tendencies that I believe threaten our success in achieving better racial understanding. The first is commonly called 'backlash.' It may be useful to distinguish between two forms. The first, which might be called *hard* backlash, comes mainly from those who are seizing the racism-on-campus issue as an opportunity to advance the view that too much has already been done for minorities. It has tones of bitterness and anger, and it can be deeply disturbing. But it is not hard to recognize, and even easier to reject. Thus it poses a far less serious threat than a softer, subtler form of backlash: the disaffection of those who have believed in and have fought for equal opportunity and full minority participation. Too many of them, I fear, are concluding that they aren't wanted, and that they should expend their energies for social improvement in other ways. That would be a tragedy; we need them, and we won't have them unless, as I said earlier, they can be made to feel part of the solution instead of treated as part of the problem.

"That relates closely to the second threat. Time and again we have seen the promotion of racial understanding linked to a more focused—and less broadly understood and accepted—political agenda. That kind of load is probably too heavy for a delicate structure to bear all at once. This fall, for example, some entering students who would have been ready to commit themselves enthusiastically to new cultural understandings were turned off by the advice that they adopt, along with them, positions on everything from a complex local labor negotiation to the national election. Nothing, to be sure, can be entirely free of politics, but too much is too much. Nor is it readily understandable to many students why racial incidents are so frequently followed by demands that bear little relation to the circumstances or the envi-

ronments in which the incidents took place. Freeing our goal of
racial understanding from this heavy political weight would, I
think, make it easier to achieve—and also reduce the possibility
of backlash.

"Much more could be said, obviously, on all of these topics. I
trust it will, because this is a dialogue that should engage this
community on a continuing basis if we are to make the progress
we need and want. What I hope we shall have, if that progress is
forthcoming, is a mature multicultural community characterized
by a kind of robustness as well as by sensitivity. What do I
mean? I mean that it will not only be a caring, constructive,
learning society, but also one with the confidence and strength
to withstand, and then to progress beyond, the infrequent but
inevitable lapses it will experience. We are clearly not there yet,
but it is an objective we can attain—and in doing so, give others
a glimpse of what the future can be like."

Naturally, the concerns of various minority communities focused on what specific steps "the university" was going to take
to restrict and to punish racist acts or statements. Proposals were
developed for the Student Conduct Legislative Council, the body
responsible for interpretations of the Fundamental Standard—
Stanford's old and rather loose governing standard for student
conduct. Early versions contained provisions that looked to
many like impermissible curtailments of free speech. Under the
leadership of Professor Tom Gray of the Law School, these were
more carefully crafted in an effort to stay within the constraints
of First Amendment protection. But of course not everyone
agreed that they had—not even all members of Stanford's distinguished guild of constitutional law scholars.

The ensuing campus-wide conversation was one of the finest
exercises in general education about a vital principle that I have
ever seen. There were many letters in the *Daily* from thoughtful
faculty members and students. There was a debate among four
Stanford law professors before a large audience. Repeated drafts
of what became known as the Gray Proposal were subjected to
criticism. Eventually, a recommendation was produced. I wasn't

fully satisfied with it, though it passed muster with the student and faculty legislative bodies. Under Stanford's rules the President may set aside a recommendation if extreme circumstances warrant it. I decided that this was an important prerogative of the community: it ought to have the right to try out a rule and then, if it decides it doesn't like it, force the development of another. The SCLC rule, unlike several other "hate speech" rules passed on other campuses, was felt by many to give proper respect to First Amendment principles—though it has since been ruled against in an external legal proceeding. But others believe that *any* such efforts to limit speech are inimical to the kind of atmosphere that ought to be the hallmark of a university campus.

Free speech also became an issue, though surely in a more frivolous context, in a skirmish that arose over—of all things—a file accessible on the university's computer system. We received a number of complaints about one of the seemingly limitless repertoire of joke files. Called "rec.humor.funny," it contained jokes that were—I looked for myself—sexually and/or ethnically highly offensive. I thought the complaints had merit, and wondered why we were subsidizing such stuff. When it was announced in the Senate that I was considering scrubbing the file, the complaints could be heard far and wide on the Internet and elsewhere. One faculty member in the Computer Science Department charged that it was the equivalent of censoring books in the University Library. It seemed to me that this was like arguing that notices placed on the Coke machine in the library attained, by virtue of their location, the status of books. After one or two stormy sessions in the Senate, it turned out that deleting the file was technically extremely difficult to accomplish without getting rid of really valuable stuff. We gave up on the effort, though unconvinced by the "censorship" argument.

The problems associated with racial difference returned to the forefront shortly afterward, in May. Just before Commencement in 1988, a committee addressing race relations at Stanford—the University Committee on Minority Issues—had submitted a report. We began a rather complicated area-by-area review process in 1988–1989, and in the Spring Quarter I was ready to announce a number of initiatives in my annual report to the faculty. There had been some signs of impatience on the part of minority students with the time we had taken, but nothing I saw had indicated any basis for expecting a confrontational action. But we got one, the day before my scheduled appearance before the Academic Council, in the form of an early morning takeover of my office. The following quickly prepared account of those events was added to my report.

"Unfortunately, I now must turn to a more somber subject. Even as I was preparing this report in my office on Sunday, others were apparently preparing to seize that office early Monday morning. My account of the subsequent events naturally depends upon information and observations communicated to me by others, mainly members of my staff.

"At approximately 7:45 a.m. on Monday, the protesters gained entry by a well-planned ruse perpetrated on a receptionist. A student leader known to, and trusted by, the staff in Building Ten was admitted on the basis of a misrepresentation of her intentions. She then helped others force their way into the building. Later the receptionist and another member of my staff were evicted in a way that can only be described as menacing. Telephones were unplugged and doors barricaded with two-by-fours and chains brought for that purpose. Communications and work essential to the function of the University were disrupted for more than a day, and the confusion and discontinuity will take much longer than that to repair. The direct cost to the institution was great, though perhaps not so great as other costs to which I shall refer in a moment.

"Several principles governed our response to this disruption. They are not new principles; they are the same ones that were in force during the administration of President Lyman, and that have been continued in this one. First, institutional processes must be restored as soon as is consistent with the safety of students and others. Second, no negotiation or discussion of substance will take place in response to unlawful coercion. Third, we do *not* suspend our willingness to talk and work toward solutions when those discussions have an origin outside the coercive context. Fourth, we *do* discuss with protesters their options and the consequences of their actions, so that they can make well-informed personal choices according to their own convictions. Fifth, the consequences of those choices follow—that is, whatever sanctions are prescribed by outside laws and by campus policies will proceed.

"We followed these principles carefully in the present case and will continue to do so. Vice President and General Counsel John Schwartz and Director of Public Safety Marvin Herrington directed the University's responses on the scene, and I was in frequent communication with them. Several concerned faculty and staff members were given access to the occupied building, and numerous efforts were made to persuade the occupants to leave. Commitments to later discussions on my own part were offered and rejected. The decision to make arrests was not a matter of first, but of last resort, and the Stanford police handled a very difficult task with admirable restraint and professionalism.

"When the arrest protocols specified under the Sheriff's policies had filled a police bus with arrestees, the bus was illegally blockaded, and a potentially dangerous crowd situation resulted. Arrangements were then made so that the protesters could be cited and released at the scene rather than at the jail or the police station. As a result the danger was averted. The protesters have claimed that this result was a 'victory.' Indeed it was—a victory of restraint and of good sense.

"I have told the press that I was surprised both by the occurrence and by the style of this disruption. The occurrence surprised me because it intercepted a process that was consensual and that, I thought, deserved and enjoyed general if not universal respect in the Stanford community. The style surprised me because it suggested a willingness to engage in threats and interference that I have not seen at Stanford during this decade. And I was also surprised at the few individuals who, once the occupation was established and public attention had been focused on it, were prepared to ignore or forgive these facts, and to lend their direct or tacit support to an unfortunate and illegal venture. Despite these feelings, I have agreed to meet on Monday with ten representatives of the student group supporting the Agenda for Action in order to hear their views.

"To all this I cannot help but add one more concern. Over the past two years, pride in this university has put energy and enthusiasm behind our representations, to the world outside, of the Stanford community as one in which an ambitious progressive spirit coexists with a commitment to reason.

"We have asserted that claim on Stanford's behalf in response to various external attacks on our processes—attacks in which we have been accused, for example, of changing our curriculum in response to coercion. Many of you on this faculty have been wholehearted participants in this more reasoned process, including some who had deep reservations themselves about the changes that were being made. I thank you for that. But today, we have to ask ourselves how much damage has been done to our credibility. I fear that the events of this week have wrought heavy damage, and may have rekindled doubts among our friends as to whether we are a community dedicated to rational process and deserving of their respect. And I think particularly of other institutions that may have sought in us a model for change, and may now wonder whether we are worth imitating after all.

"So, my friends, we now face a challenge: that of repairing and restoring confidence, while still pressing ahead with the vision I believe most of us share. I promise you that I am ready to put aside my own disappointment and begin, and I hope I will be joined in the task by all who love Stanford."

We were insistent that prosecution of the arrestees be determined by the District Attorney without Stanford intervention, though we did hold several conversations with the protesters— partly, I must say, to discover why they had done such an unexpected and fruitless thing. Their accounts were various—some evidently sincere, some confused, some unforthcoming. We learned later (in part due to an unusually thorough piece of investigative reporting by the *Daily*) that there was a significant outside influence on the plan by a statewide organization called the League for Revolutionary Struggle. But many of the protesters were obviously unaware of that, and deeply concerned with the issue of how we could improve the Stanford environment for minority students. Our determination was to let the consequences of actions flow, but at the same time to bring some sympathetic understanding to the underlying motives. In the end, I thought it produced the best outcome possible from an ill-considered action.

One other framework for that year exists, at least in my own memory of it. It is impossible to be a part of Stanford for three decades—at that time, very nearly a third of the University's existence—without developing an interest in, and respect for, its extraordinary history. The then new and already highly successful Dean of Memorial Church, Bob Gregg, did the unexpected thing of asking me to preach a sermon on Founders' Day. I overcame my religious inadequacies by resorting to an historical contrast between the issues that beset Stanford (and America) today and those that Leland and Jane Stanford might have predicted.

"As a person not devoted to a particular theology I have no ordered sense of sacredness about this occasion, save one: I have been raised to believe that the pulpit has significance, and that it is meant for the expression of deeply held personal belief. Thus I feel obliged to transmit some of mine, and since it is Founders' Day I shall be right in the tradition of the times if I am mildly homiletic.

"Founders' Day is always an important day for Stanford, and surely its celebration gains added significance as we approach the University's Centennial with what must seem to some like exquisite stealth.

"At such an anniversary one inevitably begins to think about change. I did, in starting to prepare for this occasion, and I found myself reflecting upon our own history of change, in the form of a little series of dialogues with the Founders. Imagine that Senator and Mrs. Stanford are here with us, part of the congregation in this church that they built in memory of their dead son. What do we have to tell them, in just a few words, about what has happened in the short history of the university they founded? (If it doesn't really seem short to you, it may help to establish a personal link with those days. For example, I remind myself that my father, doing just fine on the coast of Maine this morning, was also alive and well as the Stanfords watched the first four-year class of students graduate in 1895.)

"We might start with these few stories, as we turn to Leland and Jane Stanford and try to make them understand how different things are.

"'Senator, the loggers of your day took trees from perhaps a few thousand acres of land a year. In South America today, in regions of rain forest so rich they would have amazed your friend Jordan, a thousand times that much land is being stripped of its vegetation each year, and other great areas are being burned by fires so vast that their smoke can be seen from satellites. (Senator, we'll have to tell you about the satellites some other time.) Some of this destruction is being carried out by rich men, who want to get richer. This you might understand, though you would perhaps be astonished by the scale. But some of it is being done by poor men, who want merely to keep themselves and their families alive.'

"'Mrs. Stanford, we are anguished by a disease that may have arisen in Africa, and that has jumped around the world more rapidly than any plague—in a pattern related to the arrangement of great international airports. (We'll explain airports to you later, Mrs. Stanford.) At your university the disease is being studied by noted scientists who have developed an unprecedented way of doing research on it in animals, but their work is running into difficulty because some believe we shouldn't be doing anything with the animals. Meanwhile students at Stanford—fine young men and women of whose values and conscience you would otherwise approve—are counseling one another on safe ways of having sex without contracting this disease.'

"Well, you too could take a moment to reflect on how you would explain your deepest concerns about contemporary life to Leland and Jane Stanford on Founders' Day. It is one way of getting a fix on the pace of change.

"But I suspect we all recognize the central change that is sweeping our world into its next century. There are too many people in it, and its resources are very inequitably distributed among them. From that, much else follows: poverty, massive species extinctions, the arms race, global warming, and so on.

"That news would pose a very special problem for the Founders. When they established this institution nearly a century ago, Leland and Jane Stanford surely believed they were bringing a civilizing influence to a frontier, and supplying some tools for coping with its central problems: isolation, aridity, technological backwardness. How different things seem now: the major challenges with which Stanford University is helping our society cope have to do with too many people, not too few. And that striking pace of change is accelerating. The life cycle of buildings, products, and conventional wisdom is shrinking fast, and our roster of Most Pressing Problems is transforming before our very eyes: Sputnik becomes Honda, nuclear winter becomes greenhouse effect, and the dust bowl becomes the rust bowl and then, quite magically, the dust bowl again.

"All of this comes from the increased interaction rate of people, and everything that derives from them. Culture, information, all the artifacts of human life are moving and colliding with a frequency and a momentum that would have amazed the Founder. As the volume and the pace of activity rise, the internal friction of our existence rises too. And as our interactions become more self-canceling and defeating, we can be forgiven for wondering whether we are not lowering ourselves by our own bootstraps.

"Well, the Stanfords might be bewildered by all this change, but they created the one kind of institution that ought to be able to deal with it. It is likely that Leland Stanford thought the way you dealt with great problems was to grow your way out of them. But the trouble with the great problems of this kind is that you just can't solve them in that way. Indeed, growth is precisely the wrong solution—unless the growth is in an institution that supplies knowledge and information and power to change the inequities that will cripple the human venture if they are not solved. Perhaps without ever understanding why, Leland and Jane Stanford created just the right institution for a world they could not possibly have foreseen. They provided that it would be rich in knowledge, and insisted that it ought to make that knowledge available for societal improvement.

"That makes our setting a profoundly challenging one. We are, or should be, at the very source of change—where new understanding is used to empower the less fortunate. It is to be expected that we are at the center of controversy, and we find that we are not disappointed. It is to be expected also that we are at the confluence of great forces—some wishing us to retain the state of things, some hoping that we will be agents (indeed, agents provocateurs) of change. We are not disappointed in that, either. We are a battleground—but after all, we volunteered for it.

"So life in our university community, like the life of the future, is characterized more by uncertainty and instability than by anything else. In that respect our institutional life is no ivory tower, but a more accurate version of our society's next life than we can find in the more familiar and stable elements that surround us.

"Living and preparing for such a life is what I want to talk to you about. It is not easy. I actually began thinking about this sermon under the title, believe it or not, of 'Moral Imperatives for a Changing World.' That is a pretty pretentious mouthful, and it is a credit to Bob Gregg's tolerance that he kept a straight face when I shared it with him. I confess this not to seek the kind of sympathy that is born of relief, but because it reflects my determination to talk about the difficult subject of morality as well as my conviction that change is the most significant reality of our future lives.

"I discarded the idea because after I had thought for a while about the phrase 'moral imperatives,' I decided I didn't like it at all. An imperative comes before anything else; and in a world of change, in which you don't know what's coming, an ironclad top-value priority is likely to be wrong or useless much of the time.

"A second reason, even more convincing to me, is the evidence that the holders of such beliefs readily turn into zealots when conditions and rules are abruptly altered. Zealotry, a recent analyst of the Rushdie affair observed, is a wildly self-protective reaction that rises acutely when people feel they have lost control of their moral environment. How ironic it is: the most high-sounding moral assertions result from the highest level of moral insecurity. Viewed in this light, 'moral imperative' is an oxymoron, like swift justice.

"As a reliable guide to changing times and circumstances, there is something far preferable to a canon of moral imperatives. It is the kind of functioning morality that doesn't express itself through imperatives, but relies on guidelines and principles—just the sort of tools that work best in the face of unpredictability. There are some familiar examples.

"Hippocrates had it right: he led off his list of moral precepts for the practice of medicine with the aphorism 'first do no harm.' This practical bit of wisdom recognizes that even in a sick organism (or a sick society) intervention is at least as likely to be bad as to be good.

"The Golden Rule is pretty useful, too. It is called a rule, but there is nothing imperative about it. It is called golden, I suspect, because its greatest effect is not on the recipient but on the doer. If you doubt this proposition, look for those people who practice it so habitually that they have accumulated legions of secret beneficiaries. They are almost all happy people, because they have been following a guide to sensible human conduct that works for them, and under widely varying circumstances. There is a corollary that is particularly important for those who bear responsibility for institutions: one should be judged on the basis of actions and not assertions. You cannot transmit moral values you do not yourself possess and exhibit. For someone to say 'We believe in the fair and equitable treatment of our human resources in this organization' avails nothing if the speaker engages in unfair or inhumane conduct.

"Perhaps we should call such guidelines moral *assumptions*, because that is what they really are. I want to talk about three of them. First, free and individual choice is much to be preferred over compulsion. Offer incentives to people to make the right choices freely, rather than offering them punishments for making the wrong ones. Jeremy Bentham referred to 'puppy dog laws'— ones that offer little guidance and rely on an aggregated record of spankings to guide future behavior. 'Don't pollute' is a vague and arbitrary dictum. I always preferred the old Czech law for clean rivers: your intake should be located downstream from your outfall.

"Second, the most morally meaningful actions are the ones that are closest to home, most personal. All politics is local politics: the most moral behavior is local behavior. A lot of zealots in the late 1960s who knew exactly what was required to fix the world forgot that fairness and decency begin in your own community, and they temporarily lost their souls.

"Finally, the best moral assumptions start with human worth: people are mostly good. They are even better when you expect a lot of them. In this respect, trust is the most useful principle of all—it provides enormous incentive to the trusted person, it offers welcome efficiency to the person who trusts, and it provides the most economical basis on which to organize social relationships. Indeed, societies that feel they cannot afford it have already given up, for when trust fails as a moral assumption it is quickly replaced by an increasingly long list of moral imperatives. Societies to which this happens soon find that they have become helplessly stiff in the face of change.

"Fortunately, the Founders gave us a university, and thus a community, that was based from the beginning on trust, and we have preserved it in just that way. That way demands a certain flexibility and capacity for forgiveness, for whatever its advantages trust is imperfect in that inevitably it is occasionally disappointed. But a resilient and trusting community can withstand those lapses, knowing that it has the strength for risk-taking and that it can manage the change in its future.

"Of all the institutions we have, the kind the Stanfords founded here is the most fitting object of Isaiah's announcement: 'Behold, I am doing a new thing: now it springs forth, do you not perceive it?' We court and expect change; and we need to be prepared to live comfortably with it.

"Moral imperatives are no way to prepare for our uncertain and sometimes frightening future. But we can move toward it confidently with a workable set of moral assumptions, among which the most central surely is trust. For Stanford it is especially central; here is a last dialogue for the Founders.

"'Leland and Jane Stanford, do you realize that your university has withstood two hot world wars and one long cold one, dreadful regional conflicts, multiple threats of human extinction, a dozen changes in national government, an earthquake, two stock market crashes, and a student revolution—and that despite all that, it still lives by your Honor Code and now is only just considering, hesitantly, a modification of your Fundamental Standard? Isn't that remarkable testimony to the durability and the usefulness of moral assumptions in changing times? And doesn't it provide you great reassurance about the care we are taking of your legacy?'"

In a year in which students had experienced strong and often clashing views on important issues, ranging from curriculum through race relations to campus disruptions, it would have been natural to select balance as a theme for a benediction. An even more compelling reason, it seemed to me, was the increasing pressure of academic and even extracurricular life on Stanford students. People were working harder than ever—on their studies, in drama, in athletics, in whatever other activity they became committed to. It seemed to me that they often expended their energies too episodically, and often responded to the needs of some outside agency while forgetting their own. The weight of external expectations clearly played a role in this, and I thought it likely that the frantic pace of professional apprenticeship practiced in law firms, consulting organizations, medical residencies and the like deserved some criticism.

And now, it is my privilege to say a personal farewell to the graduates—not only to my friends in the Class of 1989, but also to those who have worked so hard, in the diverse academic corners of this University, for advanced degrees. It was one of Stanford's founding principles that research and graduate training should not be held at a distance from what was known in those days as the "college experience"; rather, Stanford was thought of from the beginning as one university. So I begin by congratulating all of you together.

For some years now I have used this space in the program to address the timeless and troublesome question: "Is There Life After Stanford?" It is a lot more enjoyable for some of us to ponder than its more preoccupying version: "Is there too much life during Stanford?" But the main reason I like this custom is because it gives me an opportunity that comes rarely: to deliver some personal—even avuncular—advice, not about particular issues or problems, but about matters more essentially human.

"Is there life after Stanford?" is one of those questions that suggests others. The one on which I want to focus with you today is "what kind of life?" I suspect that most of you have been engaged with that question in one way or another for several years. You have, after all, been hard at work at some academic, professional or preprofessional discipline; or you have been choosing a major, or changing it once, or twice, or maybe even more; and probably you have been struggling with the question

whether those academic decisions will really have very much to say about how you lead your life occupationally. I hope you won't be discouraged by the news that, if past is prologue, what you've chosen to emphasize here academically is a fairly lousy predictor of what you will be doing twenty years from now. That's not bad news; it speaks more to life's spice and variety and its propensity to produce the unexpected than it does to any failure of choice on your part. And the good news is that you have had the kind of education that will make you receptive and intellectually adaptable to a mid-voyage change of course—the kind of education, it has been said, that takes over where train-ing leaves off.

But it really isn't occupational or vocational life that I want to spend my time on this morning. It is the life we all live in the round: as individuals on the one hand, and members of a society on the other; as the occupants of professional niches in one part of life, and personal ones in another; as givers and takers; chil-dren and parents; learners and teachers—in short, as occupants of all those roles we have in this rich, demanding, and confusing culture.

In the kind of world most of you will inhabit, the single per-sonal quality for which you will have the greatest need is bal-ance. We are overloaded with stimuli—called by a whole array of social, familial and personal imperatives. It is hard to avoid responding with a kind of selective excess—specializing one's interest or commitment in response to some particularly com-pelling call, to the exclusion of others. As I've said in other contexts, I believe this is especially visible in our national po-litical life, to the point of becoming a kind of disease: multiple infections of highly concentrated special interests, ravaging the body politic. The problem—overcommitment leading to zealotry, and to a focus on one single matter to the exclusion of all oth-ers—is by no means confined to the political arena. It is a basic human problem, and it affects all the domains of human inter-action. Some restraint and reserve about such commitments en-

able one to measure them, and one's own capacities, more carefully.

In other ways as well, balance in life has a lot to do with moderation. For example, each of you has just been through an experience in which a great deal has been asked of you. Your time and energy have been heavily consumed by obligations whose general character has been shaped by others, obligations you were more or less required to fulfill. That kind of commitment, and the intensity that often is brought to bear as a result of it, can lead to the work hard, play hard solution—one in which concentration on a requirement is followed by periods of equal concentration on one's own choice of pleasure. Kept within reasonable bounds, that alternating pattern can be an adaptive personal solution. But it is important to remember that oscillation between different forms of excess is not balance.

A second kind of functional balance is especially worth mentioning in an academic society, perhaps particularly one in California. It is the old one between mind and body, symbolized by the doctrine "mens sana in corpore sano"—a sound mind in a sound body. It sounds like balance, all right. But that aphorism originated at a time when many people were ignoring their health in the pursuit of other accomplishments: it was itself an exhortation to balance lives by returning to them a healthy amount of physical activity. Our contemporary passion for health and fitness, particularly in this part of the world, may have led to the reverse problem. Too many well-educated and otherwise sensible people are inordinately concerned with their physical well-being. But a buff body containing a flaccid mind isn't worth much to the world. Some of the people I worry about in this respect are also doing lots of other "right things": getting the "right jobs," buying the "right equipment," frequenting the "right restaurants," as well as attempting the perfect body. These people seem to me to be in the act of inventing themselves, and I wonder whether in the process they haven't forgotten to furnish their souls.

What are the great challenges to attaining balance in one's own life? I think they have to do with some fundamental distinctions about the way we gain satisfactions and the way we display commitments.

The first is that most fundamental distinction between the private self and others—whether other individuals or the society in the larger sense. It is clear that people who have no time for themselves have no worthwhile time for others: that commitment to an entirely external set of values or needs is misguided, and likely to turn into mindless ideology. It is easy, in the rush of conviction or the compulsion of external need, to forget to tend your own needs, and thus to become someone else's instrument. Balance in this area requires the investment of time in oneself: it demands vacations from the demands of others, even loved ones, and it requires serious intermittent reexamination of one's own beliefs and commitments. It may even require change of scene, or other aids to introspection. You will learn to know your own. But the test is that it be something you enjoy doing alone, and even need to do alone.

A related but different balance must be struck at the boundary between the private person and the professional person. The surest test we have for the entry of a particular phenomenon into the space reserved for conventional wisdom is the cover of Time *magazine. Several weeks ago, you may have noticed,* Time *featured the "rat race." It was pointed out that Americans are working six more hours a week, on the average, than they did a decade-and-a-half ago. There is abundant evidence that we are feeling more stressed in our working lives than ever before. I can assure you that my hard-pressed colleagues in this administration and on this faculty know exactly what* Time *is talking about: everything we know suggests that the pressure of professional life here has become heavy, perhaps even unacceptably heavy.*

Now, this pressure is not arriving from some distant planet. We are putting it on ourselves. Not even the editors of Time *understand why we do it, but surely that is no reason not to exam-*

ine it. Do we really want to submit to lives that are dominated by a kind of hyperkinetic professionalism, or do we want to preserve time for private activities, for family, and for undertakings that enrich the spirit while not necessarily advancing one's career? I think most of us do, at least in theory—but in practice it turns out to be difficult to accomplish this particular kind of balance. One of the problems is that the most admired professions have made excessive commitment the work style that is most admired. Graduate medical education, for example, is exhausting—a poorly disguised and often poorly planned form of hazing. And our nation's most distinguished law firms subject their young associates to a seven-year apprenticeship of severe workaholism, a syndrome they apparently believe can be tolerated if the victims are anesthetized with enough money. It is difficult indeed to obtain any kind of balance when the introduction to the major professions so deliberately tries to exclude it. But it is, nevertheless, terribly important to try, because when balance is deferred too long it sometimes arrives heavily laden with regret.

There is another kind of balance between the personal and the external sphere. It has to do with how we divide our attentions between problems in one's individual domain and those that afflict the larger society. It is an old and difficult contest between values, one that has particularly characterized American society and to which de Tocqueville drew our attention. There is, on the one hand, a peculiarly individualist strain in Americans, one that places high value on personal choice and personal freedom—but there is also a strong strand of social concern, directed at one's obligations to society and duty to the less fortunate. Life at Stanford has afforded a number of examples of that contest, and you will have ample opportunity to work out your own place in this classic American dilemma.

I hope very much that as you have reached your own decisions, you have given appropriate weight to the unusually fortunate position in which you are placed—to the qualities of mind and the skill you can supply to help society at large. The oppor-

tunities to deploy your special talents and your education will be extraordinary. During the twenty-first century, the world in which you will have begun to assume various leadership roles will seem to have shrunk dramatically from its present apparent size. As the nuclear balance of terror fades and concerns of global environmental quality and resource relations among nations emerge, your generation will need to pay attention to traditions, cultures, and peoples that have for too long been ignored in the United States. It will be a very special challenge, and I hope a welcome opportunity for you as well.

If you are fortunate enough to possess or to develop a passion for righting society's wrongs, you need to maintain another kind of balance, a thoughtful view of ends and means. The principle I would urge on you here is a fairly simple one. No amount of conviction about an issue, however righteous it may seem, excuses a failure to follow high standards in dealing with others, especially those with whom you interact on a day-by-day basis. To permit that to happen is to permit ends to justify means, and—in a real way—to lose your soul.

For the principal message of this leave-taking, I turn back to each of you, and to the personal satisfactions you will or will not find in the lives you lead. In pursuit of those, I wish you a thoughtful and sensible balance between what you do for yourself and what you do for others, between your commitments to the world and your duties to those around you, between intellect and health, and above all, between your private needs and your public obligations. The search for balance can be life's greatest challenge, and succeeding in the search its greatest reward. It is our fondest hope that this success, among many others, will come to each of you.

And now, in closing, I turn to those unabashedly sentimental words of farewell that I associate with this wonderful event each year. They were said at another time, in another place, to another group of graduates, by Adlai Stevenson: "Your days are short here; this is the last of your springs. And now in the serenity and quiet of this lovely place, touch the depths of truth, feel the hem of Heaven. You will go away with old, good friends. And don't forget when you leave why you came."

CHAPTER TEN

Gorbachev Meets Loma Prieta

1989–1990

The academic year 1989–1990 marked a kind of watershed in the life of the University. For the second time in this century, Stanford was rocked by a major earthquake, leaving severe structural and financial damage in its wake. In the spring we were treated by the first-ever visit of the President of the Soviet Union to an American university campus, to the tune of tremendous excitement. And at the year's end, a controversy with the Government over Stanford's use of research funds was already brewing—an event that would prove as damaging in its own way as the earthquake.

At the beginning of the year, I found the problem of balance—especially in students' lives—still too troubling to ignore. And so was the concern with which I had opened the previous academic year: the old worry that at Stanford it sometimes seemed fashionable to pretend to have less serious academic or intellectual interests than one really had. I tried to put these two together in this argument to the entering freshman class.

"To assert a separate status for matters of intellect and those of community is really to insist that we cannot lead examined lives. And that would take us to a series of absurd propositions: that nothing we can learn from the troubled record of human accomplishment and failure has anything to teach us about how to get along with one another; that creative leaps of literary or artistic imagination are worthless at inspiring everyday thought and action in the rest of us; that play cannot inform work, and vice versa. It is a view so suffocating and austere that it should never be allowed to take root in an enlightened society like this one.

"There is a corollary myth, propagated in some quarters here, that it simply does not do to appear intellectually committed or even academically busy. That's wrong. You should not be afraid to bring challenging thoughts or complex ideas to the dinner table at your residence. If someone should suggest that you try another subject, tell that person to try another table. Or, instead, show how serious thought can be applied even to recreational matters.

"Here is an example. The late A. Bartlett Giamatti confounded many in the academic world when he went from the presidency of Yale to that of the National League. Some of his colleagues even wondered whether he was being true to his intellectual heritage. (You might expect that from people who actually think that the phrase 'For God, for country, and for Yale' is a crescendo.) Here is one of the many things Bart Giamatti wrote about the human game of baseball: 'Baseball fits America so well because it embodies the interplay of individual and group that we so love, and because it expresses our longing for the rule of law while licensing our resentment of law givers. . . . [Its] vast, stable body of rules ensures competitive balance in the game and shows forth a country devoted to equality of treatment and opportunity; a country whose deepest dream is of a divinely proportioned and peopled green garden enclosure; above all, a country whose basic assertion is that law, in all its mutually agreed-upon manifestations, shall govern—not nature inexorable, for all she is respected, and not humankind's whims, for all that the game belongs to the people.'

"How is it possible for a Renaissance scholar to infuse so much literary imagination and analytic texture into baseball?

Because baseball is, just as literature is, a record of the human imagination. Both are embodiments of culture, siblings under the skin. To move freely from one to another, to know the rules of translation, to experience the excitement of applying insights from one place to an entirely foreign one—is to understand the joy of mind and of mental play. You should never be ashamed of trying that game, anywhere. If literature can speak to baseball, surely you can export your own intellectual growth to the conduct of your lives together."

Almost everyone remembers that the event we now know as the Loma Prieta quake took place on October 17, 1989, just as the San Francisco Giants and the Oakland Athletics were getting ready to play the third game of the very first Bay Area World Series in history. At Stanford a group had just filed out of Memorial Church after a seminar when large pieces of the ceiling began falling to the floor. Stones falling from Old Chemistry crushed an automobile, fortunately empty; it seemed almost a miracle that no lives were lost. We might not have been so fortunate but for extensive seismic strengthening of several old and vulnerable buildings just two years before. Had Roble and the old wing of Green Library not received this treatment, it is almost certain that some students would have died.

As it was, a number of them were dispossessed. Students from lightly damaged residences camped out in tents for a few days, until it was safe for them to be reoccupied. Others moved, often into more crowded and less desirable venues. At Hoover House we had eleven houseguests for several weeks, women from Stillman whom we came to know as friends. The Stanford spirit was much in view in the weeks and months after the earthquake: people worried about one another more than about themselves, and the level of complaint was astonishingly low. Unexpected events—a 49ers game rescheduled to Stanford Stadium from damaged Candlestick, inspired artwork on the wooden arch buttresses installed to support the Quad arches—brightened the scene.

The work of recovery began immediately, but alas, the work of reconstruction was delayed over and over again. The Federal Emergency Management Agency, which is supposed to aid non-profit institutions in the aftermath of natural disasters, could not come to grips with the Stanford problem—and the problem entailed 26 severely damaged buildings and $160 million in reconstruction costs. Fund-raising for the repair of Memorial Church began immediately, and library staff were housed temporarily in modulars; now much of the Quad work is finished, the Library nearly so, and an ambitious plan for expansion and restoration of the Museum close to completion.

Perhaps our preoccupation with the damage and dislocation produced a relatively peaceful, even constructive year. Stanford persuaded Michael Spence to leave the deanship of the Faculty of Arts and Sciences at Harvard to undertake that at the Graduate School of Business. The Centennial celebration went international, to major celebrations in Mexico City and Toronto—at each of which the host head of state made a major address. And the Campaign encouraged us by moving ahead of schedule.

Ours was not the only hundredth anniversary. At almost exactly the same time Stanford was being started, Harvard was adding a graduate school to a college that was then already more than two hundred and fifty years old. The congruence was no accident, and at the Harvard celebration I talked about how it came to be that as universities, Harvard and Stanford are about the same age.

"The transformation of Harvard and the launching of Stanford were both landmarks in the late-nineteenth-century reform of American higher education. They drew their energy from two different forces.

"The first was the importation, in the late nineteenth century, of the German university tradition. Neither serious original research nor training in scholarship had been a significant part of the character of American universities before that. For such work one tended to go overseas; and even here in the United States the few practitioners tended to be European expatriates, like Harvard's Louis Agassiz. . . . The founding of The Johns Hopkins University in 1876 represented the first establishment of a graduate university on the German plan in the United States. Clark University was to follow in the next decade.

"The two great innovations imported from Germany—the laboratory and the seminar—were recommending themselves at the same time to the more creative of the already well established universities. Among these places, none was better positioned or more inclined to accept change than the Harvard of Eliot. In at least two respects Harvard was preadapted to accept this foreign graft and to encourage its growth.

"First, it had sought and promoted intellectual and cultural diversity in its student body—much more so than its rivals in New Haven and Princeton. To be sure, there was as a result a certain stratification effect, perhaps best reflected in Theodore Roosevelt's undergraduate boast to his parents that he thought his grades were the best among the gentlemen—even though a dozen other students had surpassed them. Such reminders of social class aside, the Harvard student body was nevertheless plainly more heterogeneous than the other.

"Second, Eliot's elective system was diversifying the curriculum as well, and promoting a kind of academic entrepreneurialism. This was not an entirely uncontroversial undertaking, even at Harvard. Charles Francis Adams was later to write to Woodrow Wilson: 'I consider that Eliot has, by his course and influence, done as much harm to the American college as he has done good to the American university.' But as preparation for change, Eliot had wrought something extraordinary. In an article on undergraduate life at Harvard in 1897, one Edward Martin wrote that 'there was an old Harvard and there is a new, and the line of separation is so recent that a graduate of less than twenty years' standing can remember when it began to appear. It came with the elective system.'

"So Harvard, and to an extent Columbia, were ready to accept something new, to become in the words of one observer 'English colleges loosely wedded to a Germanic graduate school.'. . . . In other places, the establishment of graduate work and scholarly research as a criterion for academic appointment were vigorously opposed, as the potential enemies of liberal culture and the college as a device for transmitting it and the values that flowed from it. In 1902 Woodrow Wilson could urge his Princeton to 'keep out the microbes of the scientific conception of books and the past,' and admire university life as one in which 'men are licked into something like the same shape in respect of the principles with which they go out into the world.' It is not difficult to detect, in this view, antecedents for the current attitude that a proper liberal education consists of an authorized Canon of Great Works of European Culture. Indeed, one can almost hear approving murmurs from William Bennett and from the Committee on Social Thought at the University of Chicago. . . .

"The years between 1885 and 1895 . . . probably mark the significant transition in the history of the American university. But as I said in the beginning, it was also associated with the founding of new universities, built on the new composite plan. Johns Hopkins was a little earlier, Clark in exactly this period, Stanford and then Chicago a little later. Collectively the conversion of one set of older institutions and the founding of no less than four new ones constituted an event of seismic proportions. It opened up scholarly life in this country. It set in motion a surge in enrollment that would not stop for half a century. And of course it provided a boom in academic employment that astonished the professoriate. None of this would have been possible, however, were it not for the Gilded Age.

"The industrial revolution in the last few decades of the nineteenth century had spawned enormous wealth, much of it concentrated in the hands of a few men. My colleague at Stanford, historian David Kennedy, has written of this period that it also generated a new doctrine of the defense of wealth—one that featured convictions about the connection between righteousness and riches, but also foreshadowed a kind of public responsibility, vaguely reminiscent of the divine right of kings, that had never been a feature of European capitalism. The association of godliness with wealth lent a kind of moral imperative to the doing of good works, and certainly no university president caught in a capital campaign could fail to find something to praise in John D. Rockefeller's famous assertion that 'the good Lord gave me my money, and how could I withhold it from the University of Chicago?'

"The year 1989 is not only the Centennial of the Graduate School of Arts and Sciences; it is also the Centennial of the publication of Andrew Carnegie's 'The Gospel of Wealth,' in *The North American Review*. That extraordinary work coincided with, and perhaps helped to explain, an unprecedented rush of philanthropy, much of it directed at higher education. Carnegie's own admonition that a man who dies rich dies disgraced led him to give away over 350 million dollars during his lifetime—that's in then-year dollars—and Rockefeller did even better by parting with over half a billion and still leaving a comfortable family nest egg. More than 150 new colleges and universities were founded in the last four decades of the nineteenth century, and most of them were private. The large new institutions, every one of them, were made possible by dramatic gifts from single individuals.

"And the conversion of the older colleges into their newly reformed entities was also made possible by the existence of this great source of private wealth. By the end of the century, reform—primarily seen in the adoption of the elective system and the graduate school—was a wholesale success, and enrollments everywhere were on the rise. The institutions of higher education were attractive targets for philanthropy as their acceptance broadened along with their mission, and the wealthy responded. Harvard's own resource base to support a broad array of scholarly work and graduate training grew rapidly in this period. By the end of the first decade of the twentieth century, that part of Harvard was so well established that it was not threatened even by the Lowell counterrevolution that attempted to return an emphasis on liberal culture to the undergraduate college. Harvard was securely a university, and it was much too late to turn back.

"So two powerful influences—the importation of the seminar and laboratory system of research instruction and the fueling of its development by fin-de-siècle philanthropy—established a new pattern. Their effect on the course of twentieth century development in the United States can scarcely be overestimated. Perhaps the most important of all was the path on which we were set for the performance of scientific research. In the 1930s, the graduate scientific laboratories in the great universities were nothing like what they are now—but they were ready receptacles for what would occur later. At Harvard, for example, a magnificent gift from the Rockefeller Foundation had built the Biological Laboratories, and physics and chemistry were well supported. . . .

"To this very special apparatus came a huge windfall after World War II. Where was the elaborate machinery for supporting American military science to be put? It could easily have been maintained in government laboratories, or 'privatized' into the profit sector. But it was not. Under the guidance of Vannevar Bush and others, it was decided to place the venture in the research universities, and to create a continuing vehicle of public support for basic sciences. That could not possibly have happened without the transforming events I have been describing. As a result, American science became the robust enterprise we have known for four decades now—two-thirds of the basic research done in universities, where the next generation of researchers is also being trained. This co-location of real work and teaching is the ultimate outcome of the Germanic graduate school, and it is the power behind the most successful national system ever devised for the sponsorship of science. . . .

"Yet there are, in addition to these great successes, problems. We think of them as new; yet a surprising number of them are old, and reflect tensions and conflicts of purpose that were already apparent in the pains of parturition a hundred years ago.

"One that we encounter regularly has to do with the endemic loneliness of graduate student life. It is a problem everywhere, not just in some places, and it is far worse in the humanities than in the sciences. A study done at the University of California at Berkeley some years ago confirmed what we all knew about that subject: many graduate students are miserably isolated and unhappy, but those in the sciences tend to be rescued by the 'fellowship of the laboratory bench'—that is, by the instrumental requirement that they spend time where the equipment is and, therefore, in company with others. The Berkeley study asked rhetorically: 'Why is graduate education in the sciences so much more humane than in the humanities?'

"A second problem has to do with the difficulty of putting breadth into the graduate experience, and the often extreme difficulty of gaining acceptance for interdisciplinary or policy studies. To be sure, some interdisciplinary fields of study have matured into acceptability . . . but their establishment is slow and painful. When there is a policy objective in sight, progress becomes glacial; there is a profound academic mistrust of the world of practice. That spirit, it strikes me, is less a descendant of the idea of the graduate school as it was established here a hundred years ago than it is of the narrowly defined commitment to liberal culture that opposed it. Some things are very, very hard to banish.

"The same can be said, I think, of the old dilemma of the college within the university. At places like Harvard and Stanford one wonders whether the grafting together of that 'Germanic graduate school with an English college' hasn't left some antibodies circulating in both parts. Certainly the struggles continued long after the definitive beginning of graduate education here and elsewhere. At Harvard Charles Francis Adams, Le Baron Russell Briggs, and of course Lowell himself were championing a counterrevolutionary return at least to the former prominence of liberal culture in the undergraduate curriculum. Hugo Münsterberg wrote in 1913 that despite the success of the German method many academic men 'miss in the technique of that new university method the liberalizing culture which was the leading trait of Oxford and Cambridge. This longing for the gentleman's scholarship after the English pattern has entered many a heart.'

"Has it ever left? We still see the signs of longing: for the prescribed and closed sets of things known; for the very same homogeneity of philosophy and purpose that Woodrow Wilson sought so energetically in the graduates of Princeton; for the intimacy and clarity of the tutorial relationship between like-minded lad and mentor.

"Surely it is time to realize how much more the graduate branch has brought to the rootstock of the college. The richness of the university experience, the opportunity to engage in serious independent study of an original kind, and above all the challenging clash of different values and beliefs has lifted undergraduate education to an extraordinary degree. And it will need more, much more, of that kind of influence if it is to be adequate to the next century. As the world shrinks and a multipolar system of relationships replaces Great Power détente; as societies, beliefs, and cultures which were once arcane and academic become critical to our existence; as the scientific issues that underlie the future of our global environment become the regular stuff of policy making—as these things happen, the breadth and special knowledge of the university become more essential to undergraduate training and to the life of the college.

"Finally, a word about a singular failure of graduate education—and here I am talking primarily of its original and central purpose, the replication of the academic profession through the research doctorate. I suspect this problem has concerned those responsible for graduate education since its beginnings. I would state it in this way: although doctoral training is preparation for a profession—one that is deeply honored in American life, albeit not as deeply as we might wish—it does precious little by way of preparing students for the profession in which they will practice.

"To begin with, we make only the slightest effort in the direction of teaching how to teach. I imagine that most preceptors in the scholarly disciplines believe in some version of the old saw that teachers are born, not made; at least most of them doubt that there is any useful body of theory or any data base that could be deployed to help convert young people from adept learners to skillful teachers. Yet that is a difficult and challenging transition at which many members of the professoriate, including some of our colleagues, fail ignobly.

"We also talk much too little about personal obligation to one's students and colleagues. What kind of human attention do faculty members owe their students when there is obvious personal distress and emotional need? To what extent is it appropriate to use the classroom for promulgating personal views of the subject matter? My point is not to define some obligations here; I don't deny the difficulty of that. But I find few faculty members who have wrestled seriously with such questions. The first question is likely to be responded to with the assertion that intellectual and not personal development is the faculty's responsibility. The second usually generates a quick assertion about academic freedom, as though that infinitely elastic concept could cover just about any degree of professorial bias or idiosyncrasy in the teaching role.

"And finally, there is little systematic attention to the ethics of the profession, whether it concerns the treatment of human subjects, the shared ownership of intellectual property, or the avoidance of conflict of interest in one's scholarly work. I think our enterprise is paying a heavy price for that: we are experiencing a significant erosion in public confidence in academic work. Fraud in university science now gets major attention from Congress and in the press. There are cases, too many of them, in which academic scientists have been so insensitive to conflict-of-interest questions that they have undertaken research projects involving blatant self-dealing. A sorry indicator of the state into which things have passed is the success enjoyed by the so-called animal rights movement in portraying academic biomedical scientists as ruthlessly ambitious glory-seekers who care nothing for their students or for healing. That a movement so demonstrably opposed to the public interest and so committed to lawlessness itself could gain even limited success with such an argument is a disturbing indicator of our difficulty. Law schools— even, Heaven help us, business schools!—are devoting more time and attention to teaching their students about professional responsibility than we who are training our own successors! It is an extraordinary irony.

"But perhaps it is not so surprising. At the turn of the century, just eleven years after the founding of Harvard's graduate school, there were only about five thousand graduate students in the country—compared to a quarter million undergraduates. Those few were mostly young gentlemen of privilege, second sons perhaps, who could be counted upon to have brought with them certain principles once firmly associated with a social class, and who would apply them confidently in an arena of the like-minded. That may or may not have been an entirely realistic assumption then. But it is surely not now. At the first-century mark, graduate education has achieved the promise of Eliot's movement toward diversity: it is right in the maelstrom of our national life, put there by its own success. It faces the challenge of public skepticism, not a new problem but an old one. It can meet that challenge by recalling that it is, after all, the child of reform."

Research was also a troubling subject. As Stanford was making plans for the renovation of its science facilities—one of the central objectives of the Centennial Campaign—faculty concerns were developing over the impact of the new buildings on Stanford's indirect cost rate. The government's rules permit the recovery of costs generally associated with "sponsored" research, including administrative costs, library, student services provided to graduate students, and depreciation or "use charges" on research buildings.

In 1990 the indirect cost rate had risen to 73 percent, near the top of the list among U.S. research universities. An analysis suggested that Stanford would have to raise the rate considerably in order to recover the costs that would have been associated with the new buildings. Objections on the part of science faculty, based on the fear that a high indirect cost rate would make their projects less attractive to government funding agencies, grew more intense during the year and culminated in three unfortunate results. The first was a story in the *Campus Report* by a Stanford staff reporter named Joel Shurkin. This piece claimed that a number of faculty members were so distressed that—according to Professor William Spicer—some were planning to hold a sit-in in the President's office. If that was indeed a plan it appears to have been only Spicer's, but the account was sufficiently colorful to attract attention, not only on the campus but beyond it. The second, apparently also derived from Shurkin's interest in the problem, was an article in *Science* magazine in which a number of Stanford faculty members expressed bitter criticisms of the University's indirect cost policy. The third, under way without our knowledge, was a series of contacts involving a newly assigned official from the Office of Naval Research. He met with the disaffected faculty members, and alerted the staff of the Subcommittee on Oversight and Investigations of the House Commerce Committee. These events were the first, almost subterranean shocks in an event just about as seismic as Loma Prieta. It would become an extraordinarily damaging and costly contretemps between Stanford and the government, one that dominated the next two years of the University's life.

But in the spring of 1990, most of Stanford's attention—and much of the rest of the nation's—was focused on the visit of President Mikhail Gorbachev. Intense excitement greeted the news that his only campus visit would be at Stanford. For a month, preparations and planning took much of our attention. Negotiations with the State Department and with Soviet officials regarding the schedule, plans for accommodating huge crowds that would include demonstrators on behalf of everything from freedom for Eritrea to animal rights, and decisions about what the President and Raisa would most like to see—these were superimposed on an already crowded agenda that included the planning for a $22 million budget cut and Commencement.

It got done. The weather was favorable, the crowds huge, and the visit a spectacular success. Gorbachev was later to call it the high-point of his trip, and he certainly acted as if it were. Ignoring the pleas of the security staffs of two nations, he plunged repeatedly into crowds of Stanford students to accept high-fives and wave the Cardinal baseball cap someone had given him. Following a seminar at the Littlefield Center with faculty he moved to Memorial Auditorium to deliver the major speech that was the centerpiece of his visit. It is impossible for me to resist reciting an incident that followed, because it is a moment I will never forget.

I had carefully prepared an introduction of President Gorbachev for the Stanford audience and the (presumably) millions who would be watching on television. The idea of actually *introducing* this particular speaker made me feel a little silly, so I thought to introduce the University briefly to Gorbachev rather than the other way around. I suppose I must have done half-a-dozen drafts, and imposed on a cheerful and willing George Shultz to be sure I had not included some unwitting diplomatic gaffe. I was well prepared if nervous, and backstage at Memorial Auditorium I sorted the essential papers in my breast pocket so as to make the text the only item, and thus readily available.

At the appropriate moment I strode to the podium and looked out over the expectant crowd in an unusually dressed-up Mem Aud and at the intimidating little red lights on the television cameras. I reached into my pocket, took out the text, and spread it out on the podium. When I looked down at it, what I saw was a guide to the pronunciation of the names of the visiting Soviet delegation. No sinking feeling I have ever had compared with it.

As best I could, I reconstructed the text from memory, ad-libbing what I could not retrieve. This is what I intended to say; it is in fact fairly close but not identical to my panic-stricken real-time utterance.

"President Gorbachev, your personal daring is dissipating the ugly clouds of mistrust and fear that have hung over us for so long. On behalf of this audience, I thank you for your role as architect of a world transformation more dramatic than any in our lifetime. These accomplishments make it unnecessary to introduce you to Stanford, but I will take the opportunity to introduce Stanford briefly to *you*.

"Mr. President, we are an institution dedicated equally to the dissemination and the discovery of knowledge. Our nearly 14,000 students, 1,500 faculty, and 10,000 staff comprise a community that is rich in creativity and in energy, and growing in wisdom. It is full of special things, like one of the world's great faculties, a 600-bed hospital, distinguished professional schools, our country's longest accelerator, and its best women basketball players. It has a history of serious interest in the Soviet Union and academic exchanges with your universities. Like your own great nation, Stanford is a diverse cultural mosaic, seriously engaged in learning to cope with that diversity. It is counted on by society for the research upon which innovation and technological growth depend, for the learning upon which human understanding depends, and for the new leadership on which our collective futures will depend.

"You will find us a community deeply respectful of your courageous leadership on behalf of freedom and world peace. In the name of those efforts and the brightening new sheen of optimism they have brought to all of us, we are proud to welcome you to Stanford."

President Gorbachev gave a splendid address, in which he declared the end of the Cold War and found time to praise Stanford's Center for International Security and Arms Control and its work—as well as physicists Ted Geballe and Malcolm Beasley for organizing Soviet-American dialogues on superconductivity. Afterward George Shultz gave him a splendid old poster from the Hoover Archives, with a Pushkin quotation on it that moved him to tears. It was a fine day all round, and no one was more thankful that it ended well than I.

Commencement, after that, might have been almost anticlimactic—but of course it wasn't. Lifted by a year in which multiple successes had followed the shock of Loma Prieta—a Nobel Prize in Economics for Bill Sharp of the Business School, a Rhodes Scholarship for one of the ASSU Presidents, Goodwin Liu, and the near completion of the Centennial Campaign well ahead of schedule—Stanford was ready for a good celebration. Along with a fine celebration, it got some inspiration from Marian Wright Edelman. After such a year, what possible farewell theme could have been more appropriate than the nature of change, and preparation for it?

And now, my friends, we have reached the point in these proceedings at which it is appropriate—indeed, obligatory—to pose that timeless question: "Is There Life After Stanford?"

Someone has recently reminded me that this is the last two-digit Stanford Commencement; next year we go to three, for our hundredth. Thus we find ourselves in a time of transition for our university—the end of its first century, and the passage into a second. But it is also a time of dramatic, relentless transition for the world, as it races to the end of a millennium. We stand at a great divide between the historic familiar and the most unpredictable future this world has ever confronted. The right question really is: "What kind of life will it be?"

Only one thing is absolutely certain: it will be full of change. And what extraordinary foreshadowings of that volatility you have had in your time here! There have been great shifts in the demography of our state and of the student community to which you belong. The class of seniors who graduated when you were freshmen was 24.8 percent minority; the one that will follow you as freshmen over 40 percent minority. You have shared in the developing awareness of an environmental quality crisis that is shrinking the globe with its contempt for national boundaries. In half a dozen communities surrounding ours, you have worked in various volunteer roles to ameliorate the interlocked and deepening tragedies of poverty, drug abuse, and impoverished edu-

cational systems. At Stanford in Washington you watched—and some of you helped—Congress and the Administration struggle with a different crisis, this one having to do with rapid changes in international trade balances and a national deficit. At Stanford in Berlin you participated in taking down a wall, an erasure that symbolized the reconnection of a divided Europe. And just two weeks ago you were involved, right here at Stanford, in welcoming—with your usual warmth and humor—the most influential individual architect of this striking world transformation.

I hope you understand the rarity of opportunities like these. The chance to join personally in such events simply does not come along in most lifetimes. So I hope that they have helped to instill in each of you a sense of the dynamism that will surround you as you build your lives. Continuing engagement with these great forces will be as important to you as it will be for the world you will live in. Thus the first thing to be said about change is exactly the lesson that these events and your involvement in them have already brought home: that it is rewarding to be a part of change. Welcoming change is not easy, as we all discover. It is more comfortable to live in homelike places, and on familiar and stable ground. Yet we cannot wish away, nor should we want to, the destabilizing dramas that are taking place all around us—or the need to keep pace with them ourselves. The environment we have tried to provide here at Stanford has been a testing ground for dealing with this kind of change. I hope it has equipped you for that, and encouraged you to join in instead of standing aside. So now, in the spirit of advice-giving that farewells like this engender, let me offer some brief passages of further encouragement.

First, what you know and how you can think are going to work for you even in drastically altered circumstances. One of the great obstacles to accepting change is the fear that one's own basic tool kit—the intellectual technology, as it were, that we all use to cope with life—will cease to be useful. An education that emphasizes sets of facts and approved lists of authenticated works may indeed prove perishable when events are mov-

ing quickly. But I believe Stanford has done better by you than that. The capacity to think for yourself, to apply your analytic skills confidently to new problems, to evaluate novel circumstances with historical perspective, to comprehend and respect different approaches—these are the vital outcomes of a liberal education. They will be with you long after a changing world has brought obsolescence to many of the "facts" you learned. Education, to paraphrase Einstein, is what you have left when you've forgotten the things you learned. I think you have had a good education of that kind.

Second, change is not only frightening but exhilarating, and full of opportunity. And at this particular time in the history of our planet, it is both necessary and inevitable. The world as we find it now urgently requires purposeful alteration; the alternative—that is, the future we simply let happen to us—is a prospect so grim that none of us should be willing to contemplate it. Environmental quality, population growth, profound maldistribution of world resources—each one of these represents a challenge that will be resolved in one way or another, either by the voluntary initiation and acceptance of wrenching changes or by involuntary participation in a catastrophe. Since the former is so clearly preferable to the latter, it should be welcomed. And you should, by virtue of your capacities and what you have been given, be among the initiators rather than the responders.

Third, try to live your lives in a way that makes it possible for you to engage constructively with change. Last year on this occasion I talked about the importance of balance. Coping with change requires the kind of confident, stable footing that comes from a balanced life—one in which there is time for reflection, for family, for compassion and nurturing. It does not come from the hot pursuit of a narrow set of professional goals. On this matter I have some deepening concerns. The number of well-educated Americans and institutional leaders who believe the eighty-hour week is instrumental to success is truly alarming. The elite professions are now levying outlandish demands for commitment upon their junior members, guaranteeing that some of the brightest and most imaginative members of society will be unavailable for any tasks outside their narrow professional sphere. That is not a recipe for confronting and managing great social change. Rather, it is one for maintaining viscosity.

There is another reason not to focus all your energy outward. Change is easier to manage at a local level and on a reasonable scale. There is an old saying that if you take care of the little things the big things tend to take care of themselves. When the world is in flux, that is all the more reason to tend your garden, love your neighbor, and teach your children well.

My last piece of advice is that you prepare yourselves well for disappointment. The most confident and capable people in this world are not those who never fail, but those who are good at recovery; the adroit avoiders of failure never take risks, and never get much done. Particularly in times of rapid change, risk-takers often fall and look foolish, but they pick themselves up and forge ahead. You must be able to accommodate outcomes that aren't the ones you wanted. They are the inevitable trials of a life lived as it should be, right up on the precipice of change.

Your visitor two weeks ago and your speaker this morning are both working on enormous, often discouraging agendas. The President of the Soviet Union knows that he may fail spectacularly; Marian Wright Edelman knows that she may not get America's children all the help they deserve. Does either of them, I ask you, look miserable? They are voluntarily creating change, not just letting it happen to them. It is exhilarating to be a driver of reform, to slip off the stream-bank of history and into the flood.

But why, to come full circle, should I need to tell you any of this? You are, after all, the veterans of the Battle of Western Culture, the agitators for environmental studies, the debaters about free speech and racial harassment, the most diverse residential student body in the country, the exchangers with Novosibirsk and the greeters of Gorbachev, the copers with drought and the survivors and rebuilders after the great earthquake of Loma Prieta. When anyone asks you if you're ready for change, tell them you've been there. And tell them you're ready for more because—you are ready.

Just as one part of your preparation here has involved intense challenges to intellectual development, another part has required real investment in the difficult business of building and keeping community. These latter lessons are as worth keeping as the others. They have been learned, after all, in an environment that is anything but an ivory tower. On the contrary, it is a more intense and accurate version of the world's next life than we find in the more familiar and stable elements around us.

These Stanford lessons about community will help you in your own futures: as preparation for change, as an anchor to basic human values, and finally as a link to that memorable time, our time together here at Stanford, during which we tried to build a small society that welcomed change—and, by and large, did pretty well at coping with it.

And now, as tradition demands, I will send you on your various ways with some words of sentiment—to remind us of the importance of this time together, and also to remind you that ties of friendship and remembrance of times past are among the comforts that nourish us in times of change. The words were said nearly forty years ago at another commencement in another lovely place by Adlai Stevenson: "Your days are short here; this is the last of your springs. And now in the serenity and quiet of this lovely place, touch the depths of truth, feel the hem of Heaven. You will go away with old, good friends. And don't forget when you leave why you came."

CHAPTER ELEVEN

Centennial

1990–1991

Because the first-year undergraduate class was the 100th class to enter Stanford, Freshman Orientation and the upcoming Centennial Celebration were especially fraught with significance for me. At the very first event of the year, I talked about controversy, advocated a certain willingness to accept and even make use of it, and discussed some of the spectacular events that had occurred at the University during the preceding year.

"It is my great pleasure to extend Stanford's official welcome to the Class of 1994—the 100th class to matriculate at this University. Although I'm delighted that you're the 100th class to enter Stanford, I'm even more impressed with some of the other qualifications you represent and the special opportunities you have. Let me mention just a few of them.

"In the first place, you are the first post–Loma Prieta class. Just about the time you were getting serious about doing the essays for your Stanford applications, we experienced a considerable shake-up around here. The damage wasn't very dramatic: no structures fell down, and no people were hurt. But if you have a 100-year history in this part of the world, it means that you have a number of old buildings made of unreinforced masonry. That we did not experience more serious loss, including loss of life, was due to a lot of foresighted investment—over $30 million in seismic upgrading and reinforcement over the past fifteen years.

"The University has suffered significant damage: we have lost the use of a church and a museum, some important library facilities, and the classroom buildings in the back two corners of the Quad. I want to emphasize that we have made adjustments that will leave our academic program just as strong and sound as it was before the earthquake. But to pretend that we have not lost anything is to ignore reality.

"Nor could anyone who was considering matriculating at Stanford—particularly the 58 percent of you who come from states other than California—have ignored the reality of the Loma Prieta earthquake. The major sites of visually dramatic damage—the Marina in San Francisco and the Cypress Freeway in the East Bay—were shown to the rest of America from every possible angle on every possible TV broadcast. Surely it must have given second thoughts to families, including some of yours, as to whether this part of California—despite its manifest superiority in all other respects—is the right place for a young person to go to college.

"Indeed, we have the strongest of reasons to believe that many of them decided it was not. For the first time in a number of years, out-of-state application rates—particularly from the East and Midwest—dropped in relation to in-state application rates. One of the things that interests me about this class is that its members have made a decision about risk that many others have made in the opposite way. So welcome to fault-land, you of great courage, and take a look around you. There isn't a wimp in sight! To be a little more serious about a risk we all live with, you will be receiving important information about earthquake safety as part of orientation. Please pay attention to it.

"A second thing that's special about you is something you share with college freshmen everywhere in the United States. You belong to an age group—a 'cohort' as the demographers call it—that is 6 percent smaller than the equivalent age group a year ago. Before long the numbers will increase again, as the children of the baby-boom generation begin to go to college in significant numbers. One of my economics department colleagues likes to point out that demography is destiny, and indeed it is. You will have special opportunities and special obligations as you move through life with this group to which you belong. The good news is that you will have more available jobs, less crowded circumstances, a larger share of whatever resources are available to people in your age group. The bad news is that you will be supporting the largest group of elderly people relative to wage earners in the nation's history. You will also—alas— surely have to pick up much of the bill for the consumption of the past decade that we as a society charged to the future. So you will have to get up early, and go to bed late. Better yet, you can plan more thoughtfully for the future than your predecessor generations have, and figure out a way to distribute resources more fairly and efficiently than we do now.

"Third, you are coming to a university—one of society's great centers of intellectual ferment and innovation—just at a time when the world is being swept over by some of the most extraordinary series of changes in its history. It will be your good fortune to participate in that excitement, and in the conversations and analyses that will accompany it. This past year, for example, Stanford students at the Berlin campus participated in the dismantling of the Wall. And just three months ago a Stanford audience in this room heard the President of the Soviet Union say 'kha-load-nah-yah vi-nah po-zah-jee nahs'—'the Cold War is over.' The dramatic evaporation of East-West tensions, the emerging struggle between the rich nations of the North and the poor nations of the South, the struggle to make environmental quality a part of the international negotiating equation, and the troubling question of whether, as national identity and sovereignty fade, we can manage the even more difficult challenges of tribalism—all these we shall confront during your time here. We will not solve them, but we *must* put you in a better position to do so.

"A part of that great pattern of change, of course, is the contemporary crisis in the Middle East. Without wishing to spoil the joy of this new beginning for you, let me remind you of another way in which you are fortunate. A number of men and women about your age are, as we speak, bivouacked in a hot, uncomfortable desert doing maintenance on tanks, not knowing when or even whether they will have to roll them into combat. That should be enough reminder not only of the excitement and challenge of our times, but of your special opportunity and responsibility to gain the tools to improve them.

"Those are some of the special things about you. What about the university to which you have come? *First*, I want to assert that we are family. Stanford is a place that cares about community, and gives members a strong say in the rules and design of that community. As a result there is a spirit of cooperation and commitment here; I hope you have already recognized it in the enthusiasm of the returning students who do so much for the orientation of new family members. There is much diversity here, and this class sets a new Stanford record for representation of minority groups. But I hope you are all prepared to be recognized and appreciated first for your common humanity and for the personal and special values each of you brings as an individual, independent of any group identification.

"*Second*, we care about you and what we do for you; and we are willing to be perfectly open about the process of change even when that leads to controversy and criticism. Two years ago this faculty went through a very public revision of the course you will come to know as Culture, Ideas, and Values. The idea was to introduce new themes, including ones of non-Western origin, into a course then known as Western Culture. Some critics believed that the consequences of this revision would mark the end of civilization as we know it. But we persevered, understanding grew, and so you will find yourselves in a carefully planned curriculum that has not discarded but enriched the Western canon of great works. And as the world changes and we embrace new differences and confront people and problems with new historical contexts, there is a growing sense—here and elsewhere—that what we did was right.

"And last spring I addressed the faculty on the subject of teaching, saying that we need to rebalance the emphasis given to teaching and research in favor of the former. I said to them: 'I believe we can have superb research and superb teaching too; and in support of that proposition I offer the example of departments, programs, and countless individual colleagues who have excelled at both. We need to talk about teaching more, respect and reward those who do it well, and make it first among our labors. It should be our labor of love, and the *personal* responsibility of each one of us.'

"This proposition is not revolutionary, perhaps not even controversial; we have a strong tradition of excellence in undergraduate education here, and are proud of it. But the reaction of the media has been interesting: some of the coverage suggested that Stanford was making a damaging confession. We live in a society, it seems, that instantaneously converts self-examination into self-incrimination. 'Aha! So you want to get better. That means you're lousy, right?'

"Wrong. There is a strange form of nostalgia around, one that has made some critics of higher education yearn for an earlier day in which all faculty members were as devoted as Mr. Chips and as spellbinding as Mark Hopkins. Well, most of them never were. As Yogi Berra said, 'even nostalgia ain't what it used to be.' In my judgment, the teaching at Stanford is distinctively better than it has been at any point since I joined the faculty thirty years ago. So what was the point of my challenge? It was simply that we could be better still, and that one of the main forces in the way of that improvement has been a relentlessly increasing pressure on faculty members to invest their time in research. So I called for, and we will do our best to provide, some help in rebalancing the emphasis.

"What is needed? First, the definition of scholarship could be made a little more elastic, to encompass, evaluate, and then reward forms of intellectual activity that relate to the improvement of learning. Second, we can modify the processes by which we appoint and promote faculty members to limit the emphasis on research quantity as opposed to quality, and to develop a greater confidence in evaluations of teaching in all its forms. Third, we can supply more resources to support the best teaching, and reward the best teachers. Fourth, we can direct a convergence between scholarship and teaching by creating more opportunity for faculty members to work closely with students at the frontiers of knowledge.

"All of these things will be taking place during your time here. Watch this space, as they say, for further news. I hope you will be knowledgeable, critical consumers of what Stanford and its faculty do to teach you. We have a strong tradition of doing well, and of taking advice in order to do even better. So, to repeat the point with which I began—we are confident enough and candid enough to state our commitment to improvement. And we are confident, too, of the capacity of this learning community to grow and change.

"*Third*, and finally, Stanford is a place that will expect much of *you*. To get the most from it you need to have a similar confidence in what you have brought with you. It is easy, in coming to a new place full of more experienced people, some of them intimidatingly accomplished, to suppose that your own ideas are inferior to the ones they are urging upon you. Please don't fall willingly into that trap. Your interest and support are worth something to many people with many different agendas. Hear them out, but don't make careless assumptions about their objectivity. Cultivate a friendly skepticism, but remember that whereas some skepticism is healthy, cynicism is crippling.

"Let me put it in a different way. You have come to a free marketplace of ideas. Because we are so devoted to that freedom, we don't control it; that means you have to be careful evaluators. Tolerate and examine the unfamiliar; even give some headroom to the absolutely implausible, if only for a little while. But be awake to ulterior motive, and resist those who proselytize. Remember, finally, that the task of those who teach you here is not to give you their ideas or their values, but to give you the capacity and the intellectual tools to choose your own. The chances are good that you have already made a fine start.

"In all you do here at Stanford, be demanding. This place is full of riches, but not everyone will get the same share. You will be amazed at what you can accomplish by asking. Believe it or not, the standard reaction of a faculty member to a student who asks intelligently about his or her work is a rush of gratitude. So don't be shy. Even if that kind of cultivation seems beyond reach, you have a right to state your academic needs. If they're not being met, ask why not. If you don't get an answer, persist.

"A final thought. You will become very important to each other. Countless pairs of you, who do not even know one another this night, will be best friends, teammates, colleagues, lovers, partners before your time is done. So approach your classmates with respect, sensitivity, and high expectations—and treat them as though you were already caring for a friendship that is as strong as family.

"Welcome to Stanford."

The teaching initiative was to remain an important theme—not only during the academic year of 1990–1991 but in the years following, as the "rebalancing" of teaching and research became a national issue for the nation's major universities. But it was accompanied by the fallout from a much grimmer and more trying controversy, one that produced a major crisis for the institution. That controversy had begun during the previous fall, reached a climax of sorts at a very unpleasant and damaging Congressional hearing in March of 1991, and was followed by prolonged and difficult negotiations with the government during the academic year 1991–1992.

Here it is necessary to relate some painful events. The "indirect cost controversy," as it came to be called, grew into a crisis in Stanford's relationship with the government, and indeed in the entire structure of the university-government partnership. As a result, some damage was done to the University's reputation, and to that of honest people who worked for it. The vindication Stanford has subsequently received, welcome though it is, will neither repair the reputations nor fully reimburse the university for the financial losses it suffered from interim penalties. So an important question still hangs in the air, persisting amidst the sense of institutional relief: what produced the premature and heavily publicized judgments that were so embarrassing to the University and to me?

They resulted from an unusual interlocking of influences: the staff of a powerful Congressional subcommittee; a "whistle-blower" who represented the government in its dealings with Stanford, but who was also a disappointed job-seeker and who became a private plaintiff against the University; a group of journalists with close ties to the Subcommittee staff; and two federal agencies. Not all the charges against Stanford were wrong, and we had some things to apologize for: some sloppy accounting, failure to examine the appropriateness of costs that were technically "allowable," and a certain reflex defensiveness in the early going. But some of the most serious central elements in the case against the university were both wrong and unfair, and the way in which they became so firmly implanted and so damaging is a cautionary tale worth telling.

In late June of 1990, Stanford was still recovering from the Gorbachevs' visit and from Commencement. One afternoon Bob Byer, Stanford's Dean of Research, came into my office to tell me that the Office of Naval Research's Resident Representative was very unhappy and was claiming that Stanford was "ripping the Government off." At his urging I met with the ONRRR to see what was troubling him. Over a cup of coffee in my office, Paul Biddle and I had a friendly conversation; he made some rather vague and rambling complaints about his points of contact with the Controller's Office, but showed none of the righteous hostility that characterized his later discussions with the press. I listened, gave him a different port of call at Stanford for his concerns, and asked him to bring any difficult issues to me.

Shortly afterward we learned that a reporter for the *San Jose Mercury News* had filed a Freedom of Information request with the Office of Naval Research to obtain correspondence concerning indirect costs at Stanford. We made a similar request to find out what was going on; later we learned that contact was already well established among Biddle, the *Mercury News* reporter, and the staff of the Subcommittee on Oversight and Investigations of the House Commerce Committee. And in August we got a letter from the subcommittee's Chairman Dingell informing us that he had asked the General Accounting Office to undertake an investigation of indirect cost accounting practices at several universities, starting with Stanford.

Soon the GAO team arrived for its pre-engagement briefing, for which we prepared a careful accounting of how we handled indirect costs. I thought a tough but fair experience in regulatory oversight was in prospect, but much more alarming news soon arrived.

The "scandal" segment of the story began with the most spectacular item: the yacht *Victoria*. An investigator with the Dingell staff arrived on campus soon after the GAO team. She was shown around campus, after which we met in my office. She made what struck me then as an odd remark: she asked about "Stanford's yacht." I said I didn't think we had one, whereupon she said one had been shown to her on a tour of Alameda. We joked about it for a minute; but she knew much more than she was saying, as we would soon find out.

We commenced an inquiry, and eventually discovered that as a gift for the sailing program the Athletic Department had indeed received a vessel that *was* berthed in Alameda. The Controller's Office was then asked whether any charges connected with it had found their way into any indirect cost pools.

Indirect costs are those costs associated with research that can't be charged to particular projects. By government rules such costs are reimbursed to universities: they include those incurred because of research use of the library, administration of the departments and the central university, utilities, and so on.

They are calculated by creating "pools" of costs associated with each function, and then determining the fractions of each pool due to research and to instruction. The library, for example, is used by undergraduates for course work, but also by graduate students and professors in connection with government-sponsored research projects. A cost study is done (it might involve counting the different types of users) to determine the proportion of all library costs that are attributable to research. These studies are carefully reviewed by the government at the time of negotiation, and the resulting allocations are audited after the year is over. But errors are inevitable, and sometimes accountants don't make the right call as to whether a particular expense should be put in an indirect cost-bearing pool.

We were assured that no *Victoria* expenses were in any indirect cost pool. Stanford wrote the Subcommittee and told them. Then the *Victoria* popped up in a pool no one had thought to examine, one including depreciation charges on a group of physical assets. We wrote a prompt letter of apology to the committee, which was promptly given to the *Mercury News*. The result was a page-one story emphasizing the yacht's luxury features: the headline was "Stanford Charges Taxpayers for Jacuzzi on Yacht." Eventually, these decorations became more newsworthy than the event itself, and it became established as media lore that the vessel was used to entertain administrators and that the taxpayers had actually paid for maintenance. None of us had ever seen it, and we insisted—as was true—that nothing more than an accounting error was involved.

The Dingell Subcommittee staff, helped by their media contacts, charged Stanford with "stonewalling" on the yacht issue. They professed to be infuriated by our perceived resistance; at one public meeting in Washington, a senior member of the Subcommittee staff explained that "Our motto is: If it struggles, kill it."

By summer's end, the normal complement of two government auditors at Stanford had been augmented by about 35, and there were twice as many investigators as we had professionals to supply answers. They scrutinized every invoice from certain "sensitive accounts," especially those concerning the President's residence. Every finding that might be negative was leaked to the press—especially the *Mercury News* and the producer of an upcoming *20-20* program. When I was interviewed for that program, many of the questions were based on government audit findings that had been given to network staff before they had been made available to the Office of Naval Research or to Stanford.

The *20-20* program was very hard on Stanford, but we had little time to notice. We were too busy preparing for upcoming hearings before the Dingell Subcommittee—hearings for which the *20-20* program had provided carefully orchestrated preparation. Although I had testified at over fifty hearings as a government agency head, some of them hostile, none bore any resemblance to what was in store for us. We had some difficult decisions to make in preparing for our appearance. Many Washington-wise advisers told us that appeasement was the only course—the Chairman needed an abject *mea culpa*. We rejected that strategy, choosing instead to emphasize the important issues—the importance of basic university research, and our adherence to the government's own rules about indirect cost recovery—accompanied by a forthright admission that our accounting systems needed improvement. I defended Stanford's people because I knew they had followed the rules. And I wanted to be sure that we insisted both on the validity of our agreements with the government and on the faithfulness with which we had tried to follow them. We knew that eventually our case might reach the courts, and that any giveaways at this point were likely to hurt us later.

In the hearing itself, it proved impossible to get the Subcommittee to focus on anything but the so-called "sensitive items," many of them furnishings or entertainment items from Lou Henry Hoover House—the residence of President Herbert Hoover and later of six Stanford presidents. This National Historical Landmark is a center for University entertaining for academic and other purposes—it is home to 70-80 events annually, with a total of over 15,000 guests. The President and his family live there, but there is no separation between "public" and "family" quarters. It is rather like living in your place of business: the UPS man lets himself in, makes his delivery, uses the bathroom, and leaves. The Board of Trustees, knowing that it has on its hands a national treasure as well as the University's official entertainment center, has a policy of furnishing the house to a high standard.

The Subcommittee made much of the expenditures for special events, furnishings, and so on. These costs had been part of a pool called "General Administrative Costs"—and had been routinely approved by Government auditors in the past. Because 23 percent of this pool as a whole had been determined to be research-related, 23 percent of each item was charged as reimbursable overhead. In the hearing, this statistical character of the cost pool was passed over; and each item—bed linens, repair of a closet, flowers, and the like—were presented as though they had been "charged to the Government" in their entirety.

We took a beating not only in the hearing but in subsequent media accounts, and it was a painful process indeed. The items that drew the attention, however, were withdrawn well before the hearing—and in any event amounted to a tiny fraction of Stanford's indirect cost recovery. The much larger question concerned the establishment of the overall rate, and the charge that government officials had colluded with the University to establish a higher rate than was justified. Biddle's charges were also well publicized, leading to some newspaper headlines suggesting that Stanford might owe the government $200 to $400 million.

The history of our rates and how they are set is important here. The rate is established by a negotiation, based on actual studies of the cost pools. Stanford shows that it will spend in support of research an amount equivalent to some percentage of the dollar volume of direct support it gets. Then, after the year ends, there are audits to be sure that we did indeed spend that much. The most recent rate before the fuss was 74 percent. That does not mean that Stanford gets 74 cents in indirect cost recovery for every dollar of direct research support. The rate is based on a percentage of modified total direct costs, from which there are important exclusions. Stanford has actually received a constant one-third of its total research support in the form of indirect costs ever since 1980. That is because the proportion of exclusions has risen, and that is why the rate was getting higher.

This concerned the faculty, many of whom believe that institutions with relatively high rates will be disadvantaged in the competition for government grants and contracts. Their concern deepened when we announced that we would have to negotiate for a higher rate in 1991, and in an article published in *Science* magazine, angry statements were made by several Stanford researchers. At about this time—perhaps in response to these reports—Paul Biddle had initiated the luncheon meetings with a few of the discontented science faculty members "to see if we can do something about the indirect cost rate at Stanford." He apparently received little direct support from them, but by that time he was in direct contact with the Dingell Subcommittee staff, and was telling others that Stanford was "ripping the Government off." Much of the problem he blamed on his predecessor, and on his supervisors. Thus at the time we met in my office, in the summer of 1990, things were much farther along than I knew.

The essence of this case, and of the $200 million headlines, has to do with how Stanford and the government developed their agreements about how to conduct indirect cost studies and how to do the accounting. Like other universities we generated Memoranda of Understanding that reflected these agreements. Biddle charged that they disfavored the government, and had been developed through a "cozy" relationship between Stanford, his predecessor Rob Simpson, and Simpson's superiors. In the hearing he was supported in these assertions by the Defense Contract Audit Agency, which claimed that it had not been consulted about the Memoranda. Chairman Dingell, in the hearing, praised Biddle, criticized the Navy for its sloppiness, and urged ONR to cancel the Memoranda. Soon after the hearing they did so, leaving Stanford at a provisional indirect cost rate of 55.5 percent instead of the 74 percent that had been in place. That cost the University well in excess of $25 million per year, in addition to the expenditures necessary to respond to the heavy burden of government audit requests and to install new accounting systems—to meet an evolving standard that more and more resembled that for defense contractors in the profit sector.

Even more was at stake, of course. If the current Memoranda could be canceled unilaterally by the government, then perhaps past agreements could as well. This prospect, endorsed by the DCAA and the Subcommittee at the time of the hearings, seemed to lend more seriousness to the $200 million headlines: after all, if all past Memoranda for the years of the 1980s that had not yet been "closed" by audit were to be nullified, the total cost might be that great or even greater—perhaps $400 million, as Biddle and the *Mercury News* headlines were soon to claim. DCAA had in fact left nine years of audits uncompleted, despite frequent requests by Stanford that they finish them. Soon after the hearing, DCAA took the position that they would now be audited on the assumption that the Memoranda were not in force!

While these maneuvers were under way during the months following the hearing, Biddle was in constant communication with the press about his version of Stanford's liability, about new audit findings, and about new charges against University personnel. The Naval Investigative Service was on the scene, and talk of criminal investigations was even heard. Nothing ever came of any of that. But amidst the flurry of charges and speculation, Biddle filed a private legal action against the University with the Department of Justice. Under the *qui tam* provision of the False Claims Act, citizens may file such actions and the Justice Department must hold them under confidential seal. If Justice decides to prosecute, the plaintiff may receive up to 30 percent of a treble-damage award—a huge windfall if Biddle's estimate were to turn out to be correct.

Should a government employee be permitted to use his official position to obtain information or take actions that might produce such an extraordinary personal reward? The conflict of interest seemed obvious to us, and in fact Justice had actually asked for legislation to outlaw the filing of such lawsuits by government employees. Yet despite numerous requests from Stanford, ONR failed to transfer Biddle from his duties at the University.

Meanwhile, the Navy was responding to the pressure that had been created by the hearing and its wave of adverse publicity. Rob Simpson, the Biddle predecessor who had been charged with "coziness," was fired. And Biddle was called to Washington to receive a special medal and a commendation from the Secretary of the Navy.

Fortunately, subsequent events began to revise the picture. In a proceeding before the Merit Systems Protection Board, the Navy reinstated Rob Simpson with full pay and paid his attorney's fees. Stanford produced evidence that the DCAA, contrary to their own testimony, had participated fully in the process by which the Memoranda of Understanding were produced. The Justice Department declined to prosecute Biddle's *qui tam* suit. Biddle left Stanford, ran unsuccessfully in a Congressional primary, sued Stanford, and is still appealing a lower-court decision in Stanford's favor. Stanford went to trial before the Armed Service Board of Contract Appeals to recover the indirect cost reimbursement it would have had but for the unilateral cancellation of the Memoranda for 1991 and 1992. Before the actual trial began, in October of 1994, the Navy settled with Stanford. In doing so it conceded that the Memoranda are indeed binding contracts, and accordingly closed the "open" (unaudited) years from 1980 to 1991, accepting from Stanford a token payment of $1.2 million to cover all "over-recovery." That would have amounted to about $100,000 per year—approximately 0.1 percent of Stanford's annual research business with the government. The Navy also agreed that there had been no fraud or misconduct of any kind at Stanford. The settlement put to rest all the large numbers that had dogged the University in newspaper headlines during the period between August of 1990 and late 1992, and of course it exonerated all University personnel from the charges that had been in the air since 1991.

Thus it finally became plain that Stanford had followed a complex set of rules in good faith, and that the agreements it made with the government were fair deals, fairly made. It was a fair if belated outcome. But reasons remained for deep concern about the experience we had. I knew that in a political environment as overheated as the one in which we live, attacks on persons and institutions—particularly institutions that enjoy visible prominence—are inevitable, and often harsh. But this case—involving as it did a triangular trade among ambitious Congressional investigators, a whistle-blower with a personal agenda, and selectively fed media—produced an unexpectedly powerful impact on public opinion. It frightened federal agencies into some hasty and unfortunate political decisions that might still have damaging long-term consequences for national science policy.

For Stanford I think the damage has been transient, and much lighter than we feared in the beginning. But for the health of academic science more generally, there may be a more lingering cloud, and that would be a singularly unfortunate result.

In the spring of the year, I turned once again in my annual report to the Academic Council to the subject of teaching. Pressures on the faculty had continued to mount, tenure was even more a daunting goal, committee assignments extensive and arduous, and project funding scarcer. Not surprisingly, nothing had happened to bleed off the pressure to perform in the research arena, yet the increasing din of public criticism of the "research universities" was plainly being stimulated mainly by disappointment about how the teaching function was being performed.

So it seemed right to review the responses to my first initiative, and to put in place some real devices to help rebalance the incentives. In March we received a handsome gift from trustee Peter Bing to provide rewards for some especially effective teachers, and the attention helped raise everyone's awareness of the issue. A subcommittee of the Committee on Academic Achievement and Appraisal went to work on ways in which teaching effectiveness might better be measured and rewarded.

That would have been a good subject to concentrate on in my farewell to the seniors in June, but the events of the previous two months demanded a different approach, one that confronted Stanford's problems with the government as well as my own situation. In a coincidence at once fortunate and inspiring, the Commencement speaker was John Gardner—Stanford alumnus, Stanford professor and former Trustee, onetime Secretary of Health, Education, and Welfare, founder of Common Cause and of Independent Sector, and the owner of one of the nation's truly great records of public service. One has only a very few heroes in life; John is on my short list, as the frequency with which I quote him might suggest. As much as his extraordinary address, his presence on the platform that day encouraged me to be more revealing than I would otherwise have been.

And now, my friends, it is time to consider—according to our ancient tradition—the vital question: "Is There Life After Stanford?"

All of you, in one way or another, will have to face that question. The scholar-educators among you will confront it in overheated classrooms in unfamiliar places, as they struggle with the conversion from expert learner to novice teacher. Those just hatched as lawyers will soon be reaching for 2,300 annual billable hours, while remembering what it was like—in the time before Life After Stanford—to have a life of their own. The doctors will discover that what may just now have seemed like a watershed really wasn't, and that Life After Stanford really is Endless Education. And you, down there, the Centennial Se-

niors, will take your various routes to the future, and you will
think often of how different that future is from the way you
imagined it on this day.

I hope you will all think, too, of the character of the Stanford
life you left behind, and of the ways in which it has changed you.
This community has many special qualities. One, to which you
have grown very accustomed in the past few years, is its openness and trust. As new alumni—can you believe it?—you may
soon come to realize how much responsibility you actually had
here. And there is also a lot of accountability: we report our
flaws, trust one another, and put the facts on the table. A by-
product is that whatever the issue—CIV, racially harassing
speech, indirect cost recovery or sexism in academic medicine—
we find our family differences on network television. We should
not be embarrassed at such public exposure; it is a natural consequence of institutional prominence and our habit of openness.

A related quality is the custom of learning together—not just
from the curriculum, but from living together and confronting
challenges collectively. The texts of the past are important, but
so, too, are the passages in present life that demand transformation and stimulate growth. These times of reckoning were
called "teachable moments" by Jim Lyons, and they will provide
especially durable memories for Life After Stanford.

Your time here has spanned a great divide of change. It began in the late eighties, just as our national enthrallment with
money and satisfaction was beginning to wane. You brought
Stanford a new commitment to public service. You participated
in significant intellectual innovation, through the enthusiasm
you gave to international and interdisciplinary studies, to the
environment, and to the CIV debates. And of course you were
the first Stanford class since 1967 that, in four years here, never
surrendered the Axe.

Great accomplishments, great movement. But this past
year—your last—was memorable in a different and difficult
way. It brought us a series of problems in Stanford's relationship with the federal government, and it brought to the institu-

tion we all love the sour taste of public disapproval. We cannot, even at a time of celebration, ignore the seriousness of this episode. That would be dishonest, and it would neglect the wisest of all aphorisms, that those who cannot learn from history are doomed to repeat it.

What have we learned? We have learned that despite our best expectations and despite our confidence to the contrary, we at Stanford are not immune to errors of judgment. Our pride in our management systems and our internal communication proved to be misplaced. We failed to understand that we were expected to accommodate to a new and evolving standard of accountability. We have had to own up, in short, to being mistaken about some things and failing our own standards of excellence in others.

We have followed that recognition with public apology and with aggressive reform. But that process itself has brought another form of learning. We learned that the special social value of great universities, so self-evident to many of us who have spent our professional lives in them, is not held everywhere. For some of our critics—in government as well as in the media—the admission and rectification of mistakes is not enough. This view seeks conspiracy as an explanation rather than lapse of judgment, and invokes fraud even where error is more plausible. It is a harsh and even punitive view, and from it we have learned that outside the family, neither institutional integrity nor high purpose guarantees the regard on which we had come to rely.

We need to remember that we must have the confidence not only of the Stanford family but of the society that supports us. Thus we are deeply engaged in the process of recovery and reform. Stanford means too much to us, and to the nation, to let it suffer long from human error; it belongs, after all, not to my generation or even yours, but to your children's. So we will repair the defects, and make Stanford ready for those who will follow you.

Now let me speak more personally, and from the heart, because if our tradition of teachable moments means anything, the

*best gift I can give you as you depart is a frank accounting of my
own learning in the last few difficult months. Like all advice it
comes with a warning label: the giver is seldom the perfect
practitioner. My mother put it more simply: "Do as I say, not as
I do."*

*First, you may at some time or another suffer adverse public
attention. Only then will you know how essential it is to have
and hold your own standards for yourself. If you rely too much
on the view others have of you, you will be vulnerable to the
casually formed opinion of strangers. But if you trust your own
values, you can endure harsh public criticism and even learn
from it without loss of self-esteem.*

*Second, few of us are so free of self doubt and so independent
that we can entirely ignore such assaults—so the loyalty of those
who know us best is revitalizing. I remember some words from a
prominent man who was asked, in the midst of a trying episode
of public disaffection, how he stood it. He answered, a little
grimly: "The guys I care about know." During personal crises
you become exquisitely sensitive to the rewards of the loyalty
and love of those who really matter to you—and of those in
whom you miraculously discover those qualities at the moment
of trial. Conserve and treasure those relationships; you will
need your friends—just as they will need you.*

*Third, there will be pain—but pain is a teacher and you have
to learn from it. In a speech to Stanford alumni in Los Angeles
early in April, I reminded them that I was a biologist before
taking up other things, and therefore understood the evolutionary significance of pain. It is supposed to prevent the recurrence
of stupidity. In yesterday's remarkable Baccalaureate address,
we were reminded that these painful experiences are, in terms of
self-understanding, even more valuable than the successes. If
you hide the pain too well from yourself, you may miss the lesson; and if you hide it too well from others, they may decide that
you're insensitive—or, maybe worse, that you just don't get it.*

*Fourth, your dignity is a priceless asset. I don't mean social
dignity—the capacity to say the right thing, or to dress properly*

for the occasion. There is a deeper personal dignity that takes the hard shots with grace, doesn't look for the nearest place to dump the blame, and—above all—doesn't whine. No one can take your dignity away from you, but you can lose it. It is very much worth keeping.

Fifth, and most important: please don't draw from my experience any negative conclusions about the perils of leadership. Leadership, as John Gardner told you, entails risks. But it also brings joy and satisfaction. You should know that I would not consider trading, even for relief from the last several months, the extraordinary privilege I have had here for eleven years.

The arena, as Theodore Roosevelt called the high-risk domain of public life, is a rewarding and dangerous place. Great forces are at work there—forces you can barely steer most of the time, and can never control. But there you ride upon the majestic tectonic plates of social change and popular will. As they move and shake you, you come to understand them as others cannot. Sometimes, just when you think you know them well enough to predict their movement, they knock you off your feet. Then you must recall the homily of Marian Wright Edelman's father, which she related here last year: "It doesn't matter how many times you fall down; it's how many times you get up again." Support with all your might those who elect to enter the arena with you, to share the joy and the risks. Cultivate a wary indifference toward those who watch but never play, and tolerate them when they contribute occasional blinding flashes of hindsight.

Last of all: which arena? I have one worry about your inclinations, and it emerges from many studies of your cohort of university students: it is a mistrust of government and other large organizations, and an appetite for the personal independence you associate with ventures of small or local scale. One illustration: though more committed than your forerunners to public service, you are considerably less likely to vote.

I worry about this noninvolvement with national political life, and I fear, too, that if your preferences prevail, we will ne-

glect a national need to make the big systems work better. There is a myth abroad in the land that says we can somehow get along on venture capital and smokeless information, without big government or big production. That is nonsense. We have to make ships and steel as well as software, and we can't run a nation on local or special-interest politics. We need large systems to solve large problems, like rebuilding cities and rehabilitating the environment and addressing poverty. A nation of entrepreneurs insistent on their own space will not get those jobs done.

So I urge you not to shrink from the big tasks. Don't turn away from them because they are risky, don't turn away from them because they are public, and don't turn away from them because they are large. Our society needs the grand ventures, and the grand ventures need you.

Finally, I want to thank you for all you have meant to Stanford and to me during these past years. You and I know that this is a special place, and that nothing will change that. But you should also know that in this year particularly you have brought me a great sense of pride and personal joy—the joy of knowing, beneath the smog of harsh and often distorted criticism, what splendid things go on here. More than that, many of you have brought me the gift of your friendship and support, and for that I thank you.

Whatever your views about these challenging, trying times, I hope you will take good memories of Stanford with you. To assist that hope, I send you off with words I use at this moment each year—words said at another commencement by Adlai Stevenson: "Your days are short here; this is the last of your springs. And now in the serenity and quiet of this lovely place, touch the depths of truth, feel the hem of Heaven. You will go away with old, good friends. And don't forget when you leave why you came."

CHAPTER TWELVE

Saying Goodbye

1991–1992

As the indirect cost situation developed in the summer following the hearing, it became plain that consternation was widespread on the campus. We were about to go through a serious round of budget-cutting, one that would absorb us for much of the subsequent academic year. Some faculty members were wondering whether—because in the hearing and its aftermath there had been a strong personal focus on the President—I might be a lightning rod for continued attention on the part of Chairman Dingell and his subcommittee. No doubt others, disappointed that we had not done better, thought me a liability on other grounds. A variety of views were in the air, adding up to a climate of extreme uncertainty. I thought hard about the situation during June and early July of 1991, and decided that the only way for Stanford to move forward was to eliminate the uncertainty. So, at the July Board meeting, I told the Trustees this:

"Our meeting tomorrow finds Stanford at an important historical moment. We face many problems, some of which—like earthquake repair and administrative organization—were recognized a year ago. We knew that the solutions to these would take time and concentrated effort. And entirely new difficulties have burst upon us suddenly, with unexpected ferocity and potentially severe consequences.

"As a result, we face formidable challenges: to reshape the institution and rebalance its budget, to restore the faith of its several publics, and to replace confusion and doubt inside the Stanford family with the usual confident energy. As you know, we have been working very hard at these challenges—and as you also know, much remains to be done.

"The announcement last week of our reform program on the indirect cost issue will move us inexorably forward to resolve our problems with the government on Stanford's accountability for federal funds. The resolution of these problems will be neither swift nor easy, but I believe it will be sure.

"As we have engaged these problems during the recent months, I have been acutely conscious of how distressing and difficult it is for my colleagues to labor constructively in an environment that is so uncertain and so permeated by critical outside attention. I have also been fully aware of the pain and uncertainty felt by members of this Board, and by so many others to whom this institution in so important. The Stanford family is an inclusive and nurturing congregation, and during the past months it has suffered. You must know that I have shared this pain in a very personal way.

"At this critical moment, it will not be surprising to you that I have been asking myself hard questions about the institution's leadership. What actions on my part are most likely to relieve ambiguity about our direction, to heal internal differences, and thus add to the momentum for change and improvement?

"I have used the time since our Commencement meeting to gather views on this subject. I have sought the advice of many thoughtful people, including especially some of my wisest colleagues on the Stanford faculty and members of this Board. I am deeply grateful both for the loyalty and the candor that have characterized these conversations. The warmth of the expressions of support and the astringent frankness of the criticism have both helped to form my views.

"Over the past six weeks, as I reflected on this advice, my own thinking shifted. With great reluctance at first, but with growing confidence, I reached the conclusion that I share with you now: I intend to step down as President of Stanford University at the end of the academic year 1991–1992.

"I believe in change—and the refreshing excitement that follows the recognition that change is coming. At present we are talking too much about our problems and too little about our opportunities. And, to be quite frank about it, there is entirely too much speculation about my future at Stanford. It is very difficult, I have concluded, for a person identified with a problem to be the spokesman for its solution.

"We need to banish ambiguity and to look to the future as we resolve the problems of the past. The prospect of new leadership for our new direction will help lift our gaze and renew our spirit. And, knowing the lead time that it takes to select new leadership and make an orderly transition, I think we should begin that process at once.

"In the meantime, there is much work to do. I want this to be a productive year, one that engages with the difficult work of repair and finishes it, leaving a clear track for my successor. I do not intend it to be a lame-duck assignment; I am going to make it a labor of love, and I ask your enthusiastic support in ensuring that it produces the results we all expect.

"When that is done, I plan to begin another venture about which I am very excited. You probably know that in my career as a biologist, in government, and in my few *pro bono* commitments outside Stanford, environmental concerns have loomed large. I want to help make Stanford *the* university for academic and policy studies in this arena—a realistic prospect given the extraordinary human resources already represented on this faculty and the enthusiastic interest of its student body. It is a great opportunity.

"I look forward to realizing that ambition—after I have done my best to help form a new Stanford, trimmed and reconfigured for its second century, imbued with new optimism, and faithful to its traditions of excellence, of innovation, and of community."

The result of this announcement was a palpable clearing of the air. A search committee for my successor was appointed, and new energy began to appear as we began to deal with the echoes of the recent past. The immediate sequelae of the indirect cost controversy, most of which I described earlier, continued. The aftermath of the Loma Prieta earthquake—still dogged by a failure of the Federal Emergency Management Agency to conclude agreements about the government's share of the repairs—combined with the loss of indirect cost reimbursement to produce the second round of deep budget reductions. A faculty committee worked hard with us to design reductions that would keep the quality of core academic programs intact, yet take another ten percent or so from Stanford's operating budget.

It was hard work, but Stanford's renowned resilience made it seem easier, even for a lame-duck President. It was already partly in the hands of a new team. Jim Rosse, the University's exceptionally able provost, had left—to be replaced by Jerry Lieberman for a two-year stint. Former Trustee Ted Mitchell—then a professor at Dartmouth, now Dean of Education at UCLA—joined us for a year as my deputy to help with the budget work and with the transition to the next administration. The year passed quickly, but it had a bittersweet quality which emerged in my talk the day before Commencement, at the Class Day exercises.

"I shall save my farewells to the members of the Class of 1992 for tomorrow, as is our custom. For today, I want to express Stanford's thanks for the understanding and support of this very special class, as expressed in—though not limited to—their class gift to the University.

"In this way Damien, Verna, Jennifer, and Lance and their classmates stand in the role of proxies for all the classes that have gone before, and for the entire Stanford family. In the metaphor of the ceremony we concluded an hour ago, they are the last brass plaque, but here, today, they represent the entire row. And so, equally, do the newly inducted semi-centurians.

"So ninety-two and forty-two, in this year of Centennial plus one, just about have Stanford's first century covered. It is an appropriate time for me to praise the Stanford family, and to thank them through all of you for the support it has given me during my presidency.

"I have often tried to explain to others the extraordinary feeling that binds its membership together, and as often I have failed. It is like the wonderfully funny experience you try to relate to a friend; as the story progresses and the friend is plainly unamused by the hilarious circumstances you are unfolding, you experience a growing sense that this is not working at all. Instead of the punch line, you say in lame desperation, 'Well . . . I guess you had to be there.'

"Indeed. The almost miraculous sense of belonging that overtakes one here came to me in the academic year 1960–61; it took until about midway through, to paraphrase from Allen Drury '48, in his novel *Advise and Consent*, the long, lingering hypnotic spring of the Santa Clara Valley. It renewed itself often: in the anguished discussions that took over my Biology class the day of John Kennedy's assassination; in the sometimes inspiring, sometimes deeply troubling challenges of the late 1960s; in the wonderful times with twenty Ph.D. students, all of them undergraduates from other places and nearly all faculty members elsewhere who still know and speak of the Stanford magic; in the Human Biology program in the 1970s, where a new tradition of enthusiasm for interdisciplinary work and policy studies was formed; in the time I spent in Washington learning what it was like to miss Stanford. My dear wife Robin caught it first as an undergraduate, but the magic really came to her later on, when she was a single parent with two children and full of trepidation about starting Stanford Law School almost broke: an associate dean wrote her a personal check for the first quarter's tuition, put it in the desk drawer, and told her that if things didn't work out it would still be there.

"Now for us there will be more but different Stanford magic, and we look forward to it. But what of the last twelve years—doing what no less an authority than that great gray Newspaper of Record in New York has called 'an impossible job?' I want to tell you that it has been both a privilege and a joy. No one could have asked for better support or more loyalty than I have been given. The accomplishments of Stanford will speak for themselves over the long run. The troubles of the past two years will pass, but they have been damaging, and sufficiently personal that I have often been asked by outsiders whether the travail and the pain were worth it.

"When that happens I start to reply. I talk about the faculty and its loyal and energetic rallying to the task of budget cutting. I talk about the superhuman efforts of a hard-pressed staff, of a development office that concluded a world-record campaign in a hostile public relations climate. I talk of the support of students, including an undergraduate newspaper that—to the dismayed astonishment of our critics in Washington—refused to engage in reflex bashing of the Stanford administration just because some Congressmen were doing it.

"That part my audience gets, sort of. But then I lose them. Maybe it's the part about how the Inner Quad looks in the tule fog on a winter morning, or what it's like to be in a place where most people say hello or call you Prez, or older people console football players on Sam MacDonald road after a tough loss, or fifty young people in a residence stage a surprise party to cheer up a friend, or the Band shows up to play free for someone's birthday. When I say that even in the worst moments that nour·ishes my spirit and makes me glad I'm where I am, doing what I've been doing, they look a little bewildered. So I smile, stop talking all that foolishness, and simply say: 'You had to be there.'"

At Commencement I received two wonderful gifts. One was a nice send-off from the graduates. The other was an extraordinary talk by Kirk Varnedoe, the Curator of Painting and Sculpture of the Museum of Modern Art in New York. A Stanford Ph.D. in

Art History, Varnedoe had made a number of friends as teacher, adviser, and standout rugby player during his time here—but still it was a pleasant surprise that he would be selected for the role by a committee more noted in the past for favoring celebrity, and even better when the students at this manic occasion took his intellectually challenging address as seriously as he had.

For me of course it was at once a trying and momentous event—closing out, as it did, an opportunity I never expected to have, and a time in which I felt more perpetually challenged and more productive than I would have thought possible. Now, in retrospect, it seems even more appropriate that I chose to talk about exercising responsibility—including the responsibilities of leadership.

I doubt if there has ever been a time at which more doubt has been cast on the role of leaders, whether they are those who undertake organizing roles in everyday life or assume the risks of more visible and public leadership. It is more and more common for Americans to blame others, instead of accepting responsibility themselves. A corrosive fallout from this habit is that on every side one hears doubts that it is "worth the risk" to undertake visible office: it comes at us on the op-ed page, from television pundits, and—tragically—even in the suicide note of a public official. The *real* risk, of course, is that the best people will stay away. It seemed to me that the best counterexample might come from someone who did not escape unharmed, but who thought it was worth it anyway.

And now, members of the class of 1992 and those who are receiving graduate degrees, it is time to turn our attention once again to the ancient question: "Is There Life After Stanford?"

I know what you're thinking. "His last year, our last year, get ready for some heavy stuff." Forget it. I'm not leaving Stanford; you are. We need the beds! But still, you and I have something in common. We're all leaving something we've been doing for many years, something very rewarding, something that has developed a pattern and rhythm of its own. We're preparing for change and gathering ourselves to meet new and different tests. It is a prospect full of uncertainty and even foreboding, identified poetically by Patrick Overton:

> *When we walk to the edge*
> *of all the light we have*
> *and take the step into the*
> *darkness of the unknown,*
> *we must believe that*
> *one of two things will happen . . .*
>
> *There will be something*
> *solid for us to stand on*
> *or we will be taught to fly.*

Before we get to the edge of all the light, let me remind you of the Class of 1992 how much of that you have provided, not just for yourselves but for Stanford. First, you have given yourselves, in part or in whole, to the life of the mind—to ideas and their power to transform. Nearly twenty percent of you have made the commitment to a thesis and departmental honors—double the total six years ago. You have visualized life at the atomic level, worried about the distribution of health care, turned yourselves into Parisians in the reign of Louis XIV, composed concerti, and evaluated those others have composed. You have survived those depths of intellect without serious evidence of the mental "bends"; now you know that you can confidently apply your learning to novel problems and trust it to work.

And please don't shrink from the challenge of sharing that new capacity through teaching and further scholarship if that notion appeals to you. The advanced-degree recipients seated behind you can tell you a lot about the rewards; they've finished theses, struggled with the mix of hard intellectual work and family commitments, founded new journals, and in many cases taken the time to be promising teachers as well as expert learners.

Not satisfied to be only a community of cognition, you all have built a community of creativity as well. In theater, music, dance, the visual arts, improvisation, dining-table whimsy, practical jokes—and in everything from athletics through publications to politics—you have made a special mark. We don't have the crutch of large-scale professional programs in the performing and creative arts; never mind. You have created a high standard on your own. Neither do we have the crutch of safe academic harbors for intercollegiate athletes; never mind. You won anyhow, a dozen national championships and perpetual possession of the Axe.

Not satisfied, either, with just cognition and creativity, you have created a community of compassion. You have helped make student residential life at Stanford a kind of marvel—a community in which differences are expressed and worked through, not just tolerated. You have been willing to take risks, to surrender something of yourselves in a larger interest—as through service as RA, AA, OV, or the rest of the alphabet soup of community service at Stanford. And you have undertaken the obligation to give back that falls to those with extraordinary opportunities. The public service initiative here has become a lively reminder to the entire nation that Stanford students care, and make a difference.

For all this I salute you and thank you; you have made me proud to be President of this place, everywhere I go. And that brings me to the section of this farewell that is headed "Parting Advice," because there is an aspect of what you have done that will, if you can conserve it and use it, do more for our society than you can possibly imagine. It has to do with the capacity for taking responsibility, the disappearance of which is creating a tragic national vacuum.

When I say "taking responsibility" I am not just thinking of great ventures. This is not about running for the United States Senate, or even for School Board. It begins at the micro level, with more everyday things. In personal relationships it involves taking account of consequences: understanding that actions with respect to friends or family have outcomes, and that you have part ownership of those outcomes. Responsible people take account of their own impact, don't make loose commitments, and don't start things they can't finish. On the other hand, they are prepared to take charge of circumstances, and assume responsibility for someone else's welfare. Sometimes that means stopping to help someone even when it is an inconvenience, or might make you late. Sometimes it means taking charge of a project you don't know much about, thereby risking embarrassment, on the theory that the other participants are marginally more incompetent than you are.

These illustrations are so ordinary; why do I bother with them? Because, on the larger stage, taking responsibility is becoming a casualty in modern America.

Think about it. Surely the spasm of disgust over contemporary political life in the United States is in part a reaction to our clear perception that our Congressional leaders feel very responsible indeed for their own incumbency, but take little responsibility for the nation. Yet in our disgust, we fail to focus on the serious lapses; instead we create a teapot tempest about a comically clumsy but fundamentally harmless exercise in amateur banking.

Public scapegoating in high places is now exhibit A of our national failure to take personal responsibility. Just read the morning newspapers:

Item. The administration, distressed over the riots in Los Angeles, looks for the cause—and, lo and behold, discovers Lyndon Johnson. Lyndon Johnson! Though never exactly known for modesty, he would be astonished at his ability to control events from beyond the grave.

Item. We all dislike how things are going with the economy, so of course we blame—the Japanese! When automobile executives wave that flag, we cheer—instead of suggesting that they might cut their salaries or improve the performance of their cars. When Japanese buy up real estate in Hawaii or Southern

California, we are dismayed—forgetting, perhaps, that no one forced us to sell.

Item. Our leaders, worried about the decline in something called Family Values, have difficulty deciding whether it is welfare or television sitcoms that are to blame.

These aren't exactly good models for adult behavior. Look, bad things sometimes happen, and sometimes they are our fault. No mistake is irreversible, and nearly all stains will wash out in time. But the hasty grab for the nearest excuse only makes the marks more permanent. Raise your hand, acknowledge the foul, and take the penalty.

A second expression of lapsed responsibility is a particularly political failure. It is one form of the confusion between style and substance, the substitution of platitudes or so-called "principles" for forceful, consistently expressed plans or programs. Part of being responsible is being explicit, and not hiding behind vagueness. Leadership means offering specific solutions to the problem at hand, and then being prepared to deal with the criticism that inevitably comes to those who dare to be precise. Complexity is part of modern life. Accepting it and dealing with it, instead of insisting on 30-second sound-bite summaries, is part of taking responsibility.

One especially visible form of this appetite for simplicity is the presentation of principles as substitutes for programs. This bad idea is based on the assumption that because principles are supposed to be good things people will accept anything with that label. We shouldn't. Those who tell us that admonitions to "get up off our behinds" amount to programs, ought to be laughed out of town. Mind-numbing slogans like this are the stuff of demagoguery. Untethered principles are worth nothing. The person who offers them is really saying, "These are my principles. If you don't like them, I have others."

So much for the vacant domains of responsibility. What should we be doing as a people to reach out and take it, to forge responsibility in ourselves and others? We should start with basics. There is no more fundamental or important indicator of

social responsibility than the guarantees we make to our chil-
dren. That is the form of investment by which we commit our-
selves to make the culture flourish, knowledge deepen and grow,
and our society perpetuate the best of itself. But we are not an
investing nation. For the first time in America's history, the
economic outlook for a growing generation is worse than that
for its parents. A burgeoning debt that the Congress and Ad-
ministration cannot agree to control; a Federal expenditure
pattern that underfunds critical national interests like children
and the environment; policies that have steadily shifted welfare
expenditures away from children toward older Americans; a
health care system that takes 13 percent of gross domestic prod-
uct yet leaves 37 million citizens uninsured; an educational sys-
tem no one is satisfied with—these are the indicia of our dis-
content, and it is all too easy to blame the government, as voters
all over America are doing.

But now we need to ask one another a harder question. Is
that really fair? Isn't that complaint itself yet another form of
scapegoating? Is it right to blame the politicians when we are
the ones who are demanding No New Taxes even though we live
in the world's most lightly taxed industrial democracy? Didn't
we pass Proposition 13, and haven't we voted down school bond
issues in one local election after another? We find it easy to
curse the Congressional darkness—but we have failed to light
the candle of investment ourselves, in our private economies.
Compared to citizens in the other leading developed nations of
the world, Americans consume more, and save less. Nor have we
faced up squarely to the great social challenges of poverty,
health care, homelessness, or public education. Instead we are
entranced by magical, silver-bullet solutions: for-profit chains
of hospitals in the early 1980s and now, seeing how wonderfully
those worked, for-profit chains of McSchools in the 1990s.

In short, we have met the Enemy, and it is Us; the picture is
not encouraging. But now I turn back to you, where I began—
and there is much more room for hope. Stanford has equipped
you well, or perhaps it is you who have equipped one another, to

take responsibility. You have already had much more practice than most in accepting; your actions in your own communities, as well as your instincts for public service, are admirable. I hope that in your later commitments and in those of the government you create, that experience will be put to work. Above all, I hope you will not shrink from that special form of responsibility that will require you to stand up, state the program, accept the risks, and bear the consequences. Even at their worst, and you are hearing this from an expert, they're not intolerable—not if you acted from conviction and know you did the right thing. I want to be especially sure that you hear the answer I have found for myself during these past two years. The vulnerability and exposure that came with my role, as they come with others, are not only acceptable risks; even their most adverse consequences have been dwarfed by the rewards.

And many of those rewards have come from my complex, rich, frustrating, and wonderfully rewarding relationship with the likes of you. No one who has known you as I have can fail to find hope for the future; no one who has known you as I have can fail to believe in what you can accomplish. It has been a joy to know you; and, risky though it is, I'll thank you all by thanking some special classmates who were advisees, helpers, friends, inspiration sources, or whatever. So ave atque vale, Agnieszka, Allen, Adam, Alex, Beth, Bob, Bisch, Book, Bryan, Carlos, Chris, Chrystie, Damien, Dave, Emery, Jaimey, Jennifer, John, Kristin, Lance, Marcie, Martha, Matt, Merritt, Michael, Noel, O'B, Omphemetse, Paula, Sonia, Touchdown Tommy, Verna, Wendie, and all the rest of you.

Exactly ten years ago my daughter Julia was in the graduating class, and—because she loved Stanford in an especially intense way—I wanted to remind her and her classmates that sentimental attachments are quite okay. So I said this at her Commencement, and I want to repeat it now for you and for me.

"Stanford is a beautiful, friendly, vivid place. Give a thought to friendships, to idle times passed, to the green hills behind Lake Lag on an afternoon when breezy sunshine follows a

March rain, to an unexpected surprise somebody arranged for you when you were a freshman, to the desert smell of the dry grass and eucalyptus on a hot October Saturday, to the best volleyball hit you ever got, to the dorm show, and to the extraordinary person you admired and then discovered was just as shy as you were. Reflect on these treasures and store them, because sentiment matters."

A man unafraid of sentiment, Adlai Stevenson, said these words to yet another graduating class, even longer ago and in another lovely place. They have been my own commencement coda for a long time, and they are good parting words, so I leave you with them: "Your days are short here; this is the last of your springs. And now in the serenity and quiet of this lovely place, touch the depths of truth, feel the hem of Heaven. You will go away with old, good friends. And don't forget when you leave why you came."

Index

Abbreviations, for place names, 4, 51
Adams, Charles Francis, 166, 170
Adler, Mortimer, 111
Admissions policy, need-blind, 35,
    105
Advice: in commencement address-
    es, 1–2; on confronting real
    world, 130–32; on taking
    responsibility, 212–15
Advising associates, 57
Agassiz, Louis, 109, 166
Alcohol use, 120–22
Alumni: expectations of, 98;
    increased diversity and, 34–36
Ambiguity, tolerance for, 37–38
American Council on Education,
    freshman survey by, 101
Animal rights supporters, 85, 172–73
Athletics, 113; football, 43, 113;
    mascot, 29–30; women's, 30–33
Awful Awakening, 51–52

Baez, Joan, 76
Bailey, Margery, 107
Balance, 156–60; in intellectual vs.
    social life, 162–64; to cope with
    change, 179–80

Beasley, Malcolm, 176
Bell Curve, The (Herrnstein and
    Murray), 46
Bellow, Saul, 125
Bennett, William, 125, 126, 127, 167
Bentham, Jeremy, 153
Berra, Yogi, 5, 102, 186
Beyers, Bob, 16
Biddle, Paul, 189, 190, 193, 194,
    195, 196
Bing, Peter, 198
Biological determinism, 46, 47, 48
Bache, Sarah, 59
Boli, John, 18
Boyden, Frank, 2
Branner Hall, 18–19
Briggs, LeBaron Russell, 170
Burden of excellence, 80–81
Bush, Vannevar, 169
Byer, Bob, 189

Campbell, Glen, 113
Cardinal, as mascot, 29–30
Careerism and Intellectualism
    Among College Students
    (Katchadourian and Boli), 18
Careerists: increased number of,

20–21; students as, 18, 20, 105
Carnegie, Andrew, 46, 48, 168
Carnegie Forum on Education and
   the Economy, 122, 123
Centennial Campaign, 103, 165, 173,
   177
Centennial celebration, 77
Change, 177–81, 199; balance to
   cope with, 179–80; historical,
   184–85; preparation for, 178–79,
   181
Children, investment in, 100, 104–5,
   215
Choices, 115–19
Christopher, Warren, 18, 23, 112
Clark University, 166, 167
Class Day speech, 207–9
Class gift, linked to politics, 93–95
Clerical workers, attempt to
   unionize, 15, 25
Coles, Robert, 22
College rankings, of *U.S. News &
   World Report*, 134–35
Columbia University, 166
Commencement: change of location
   for, 69; speeches at, 1–2
Complexity: accepting, 72; of human
   society, 28–29
Computers, access to material using,
   144
Courage of conviction, 81–82
Craig, Gordon, 107
Cultural relativism, 3
Cuomo, Mario, 79
Curriculum: Jewish Studies program,
   113; political correctness in, 78–
   79; race relations in, 138–39. *See
   also* Western Culture curriculum

Darwin, Charles, 46, 48, 97
Dean Fred. *See* Hargadon, Fred
Demographics, as determining
   destiny, 183–84
Demonstrations: animal rights, 85;
   minority student, 127, 144–48;

South African divestment, 75, 76,
   79, 85, 92
Development, misinterpretation of,
   60–61, 70–71
Dingell, John, 190, 194–95, 204
Disagreement: within Stanford
   community, 128–29; without
   alienation, 82–84
Diversity, 117–18; "beyond
   tolerance" attitude toward, 33–34;
   financial aid's role in, 33, 62; of
   incoming classes, 62, 105, 177; as
   institutional priority, 34–36, 37;
   opportunity for disagreement
   with, 82, 84; remaining in touch
   with, 73–74
Divestment. *See* South African
   divestment
Drury, Allen, 208

Earthquake. *See* Loma Prieta
   earthquake
Economy, 20, 53
Edelman, Marian Wright, 177, 180,
   202
Edgerton, Russ, 122
Education: advocates for, 55; cost of,
   86–92; graduate, 165–73;
   investment in, 100, 104–5, 215;
   legacies of, 37–39, 72–74, 80–84;
   liberal, 66–69; lifelong, 53, 80; as
   preparation for change, 178–79,
   181; quality of, 20; reform of K–
   12, 122–24; training vs., 52–53,
   71; undergraduate, 6, 10–13, 40
Einstein, Albert, 179
Eliot, Charles William, 166, 173
Elizabeth, Queen of England, 43
Elway, John, 43
Enabling Act of California, 77
Entrepreneurship, 49, 54, 105; public
   service as complement to, 50, 54–
   55, 106
Ethics, in graduate schools, 172–73
   Expectations, 96–100; of parents,

59, 97; of Stanford, 97–99

Faculty: advice from, 1–2; mandatory retirement of, 25, 43, 108; recruitment of minority, 138–39; relationship between students and, 6, 10–13; research opportunities for, 11; as university spokespersons, 26
Failure: with high expectations, 100; with risk taking, 100, 180
Federal Emergency Management Agency (FEMA), 165, 207
Federal government, 3; decline in financial support by, 14–15, 25; educational reform role of, 122–24; morale in, 53–54; research and, 14–15, 24, 64; tax reform by, 85. *See also* Indirect costs controversy
Fiduciary duty, South African divestment and, 76–78
Financial aid: diversity encouraged by, 33, 62; linked to selective service registration, 42; need-based, 33, 62, 105; sources of funds for, 88–89
Fledglings, maturation vs. learning by, 60–61, 70
Football, 43, 113
Founders' Day: fiduciary duty speech for, 77–78; historical issues sermon for, 148–55
Franklin, Benjamin, 59–60
Freedom of speech: for controversial speakers, 63; with online access, 144; race relations and, 140, 143–44
Freshman Orientation, 57–63; address to parents for, 58–63, 70; alcohol use speech for, 120–22; intellectual interests speech for, 162–64; for Stanford's 100th class, 182–88
Freud, Sigmund, 47

Frost, Robert, 115, 116
Fundraising: Centennial Campaign, 103, 165, 173, 177; to repair earthquake damage, 165

Gardner, John, 71, 198, 202
Geballe, Ted, 176
Generational chauvinism, 100
Ghandi, Mahatma, 125
Giamatti, A. Bartlett, 163
Gorbachev, Mikhail, 174–76, 180
"Gospel of Wealth, The" (Carnegie), 168
Graduate education: American history of, 165–69; problems in, 170–73; research function of, 169
Graduate School of Business (GSB), 49, 165
Gratitude, expressing, 39–40
Gray, Tom, 143
Gregg, Bob, 148, 151
Growth of universities, 8–9, 91–92
Guerard, Albert, 7
Gulf War, 185

Hamburg, David, 122
Hargadon, Fred, 18, 19, 51, 58, 70, 97
Harvard University: graduate school centennial speech at, 165–73; growth of, 8
Hastorf, Al, 43
Hedberg, Dave, 32
Herrington, Marvin, 146
Herrnstein, Richard J., 46
Hippocrates, 130, 152
Hofstadter, Robert, 107
Holmes, Oliver Wendell, 118
Holmes, Oliver Wendell, Jr., 39
Hoover Institution: Ronald Reagan Presidential Library and, 43, 78, 111–13; Stanford relationship with, 42–43, 78
Humanities: increasing emphasis on, 9, 22–23; loneliness of graduate

students in, 170; as secondary to sciences, 6, 9; value of, 22–23
Human nature, post-Darwinian views of, 45–49
Hunt, Jim, 123

Idealism: aspiring to perfectionism, 73; students' lack of, 20–22
Identity, necessity of formulating, 71
Indirect cost controversy, 3, 86, 173–74, 188–97, 199–200; leadership and, 204–5; outcome of, 196–97; Presidential House expenses and, 192–93; recovery rate, 173–74, 190–91, 193–95; remedying, 204, 205; *Victoria* yacht and, 190, 191
Individuality, as element of institutional character, 8
In loco parentis, 1–2, 10
Institutional character: elements of Stanford's, 6–9; leadership matched with, 6, 14
Intellectual climate, 133–34, 162–64
Islas, Arturo, 107

Jackson, Jesse, 127
Jewish Studies program, 113
Johns Hopkins University, 166, 167
Johnson, Dennis, 81
Johnson, Lyndon, 213
Jones, Landon, 20
Jones, Pat, 107
Jordan, David Starr, 7, 16, 109–10, 111

Kant, Immanuel, 47
Kaplan, John, 85
Katchadourian, Herant, 18
Kennedy, David, 167
Kennedy, Donald: childhood of, 2; resignation decision of, 206–7
Kennedy, Julia, 36
Kennedy, Page, 69
Kennedy, Robin, 208

Knowledge: growth of universities and, 9, 91–92; impermanence of, 15–17, 38
Koppel, Ted, 95–96
Kyoto campus, 113

Laetrile, 64–65
Lawrence Berkeley Laboratory, 44
Leadership: accepting challenge of, 72-73; indirect cost controversy and, 204–5; matched with institutional character, 6, 14; risk taking with, 202, 210
Learning: beyond utility, 23; liberal, 22–23, 28–29, 52–53, 66–69; lifelong, 53, 80; maturation vs., 60–61, 70–71
Lehrer, Tom, 15
Lieberman, Jerry, 207
Liu, Goodwin, 177
Loma Prieta earthquake, 164–65, 182–83, 207
Lou Henry Hoover House, 192–93
Lowell, Abbott Lawrence, 168, 170
Lyman, Richard W., 5, 15, 29, 69, 145
Lyons, Jim, 199

Maccoby, Eleanor, 107
Maclean, Norman, 80
McPhee, John, 2
Manzanita, 19
Marching Band, 15
Martin, Edward, 166
Mascot, 29–30
Math, improving teaching of, 123–24
Maturation, learning vs., 60–61, 70–72
Maxwell, Cedric, 73, 81
Meese, Edwin, 112
Minorities: as faculty, 138–39; presidential office takeover by, 144–48. *See also* Diversity; Race relations
Mitchell, Ted, 207

Moral Majority, 28
Munsterberg, Hugo, 170–71
Murray, Charles, 46

Napier, Davie, 79
National Institutes of Health, 43–44
National Science Foundation, 124
Nation Prepared, A (Carnegie
    Forum), 123
1960s: student-faculty relationship
    and, 10–11; successes of, 21–22
Nuclear weapons testing, research
    related to, 44–45

Obligation, 54, 70–71. *See also*
    Public service; Responsibility
O'Brien, Dennis, 78
O'Connor, Sandra Day, 36
Okimoto, Dan, 107
O'Neill, "Tip," 113
Orientation. *See* Freshman
    Orientation
Overseas Studies program, 113
Overton, Patrick, 211

Parents: address to, 58–63, 70;
    expectations of, 59, 97
Paton, Alan, 131–132
Peace Corps, 53, 106
Perkins, Robbie, 85
Pittendrigh, Colin, 107
Planck, Max, 91
Plaque-laying ceremony, 15–17
Political correctness, 78–79
Politics: class gift linked to, 93–95;
    non-involvement with, 202–3;
    responsibility in, 214–15; single-
    issue, 28–29, 38, 83–84, 93–95
Praise, 131
Predictions, 5–6; on life after
    Stanford, 52–55
Presidents, university: advice from,
    1–2; job of, 2, 209; taking
    positions on public issues, 24–28
Princeton University, 167, 171

Public criticism, 200–202
Public education, quality of, 20
Public service: advice on, 23, 101; as
    complement to entrepreneurship,
    50, 54–55, 106; failures of, 20–
    21; low status of, 53–55, 68;
    opportunities for, 99–100

Quad, class plaques in, 15–17

Race relations, 135–44; backlash in,
    142; in curriculum, 138–39;
    freedom of speech and, 140, 143–
    44; politicization of, 142–43; in
    residential community, 136–38;
    Ujamaa incident involving, 135–
    36, 139, 140, 141; university
    response to problems of, 140–42,
    143–44. *See also* Diversity
Research: development of American
    graduate schools and, 169; federal
    government and, 14–15, 24, 64;
    nuclear weapons testing and, 44–
    45; opportunities for faculty in,
    11; teaching emphasized over,
    186–87, 188. *See also* Indirect
    cost controversy
Research universities, teaching at,
    106–11, 197–98
Resident Assistants, 57
Responsibility, 212–15; in politics,
    214–15; public, 54–55;
    scapegoating to avoid, 213–14
Retirement, mandatory, 25, 43, 108
Rice, Condoleezza, 107
Risk taking: with choices, 117;
    failure with, 100, 180; with
    leadership, 202, 210; speaking up
    as, 73
Rockefeller, John D., 168
Ronald Reagan Presidential Library,
    proposed site of, 43, 78, 111–13
Roosevelt, Franklin Delano, 131
Roosevelt, Theodore, 166, 202
Rosse, Jim, 207

San Jose Mercury News, 190, 191, 192, 195
Scapegoating, to avoid responsibility, 213–14
Schools. *See* Education
Schwartz, John, 146
Sciences: emphasized over humanities, 6, 9; improving teaching of, 65–66, 123–24; isolation of graduate students in, 170; knowledge in, 9, 91–92; utilitarian institutional character and, 7–8
Scientific literacy, 64–66
Selective service registration, financial aid linked to, 42
Sense of humor, 39
Sharp, Bill, 177
Shirley, Robert, 132
Shockley, William, 46, 63
Shultz, George, 50, 175, 176
Shurkin, Joel, 174
Simpson, Rob, 194, 196
Single-issue politics, 28–29, 38, 83–84, 93–95
Social investment, 103–5
South African divestment, 3, 75–76, 92, 103; class gift in support of, 93–95; demonstrations supporting, 75, 76, 79, 85, 92
Speakers, controversial, 63
Spence, Michael, 165
Spencer, Herbert, 46
Spicer, William, 174
Sports. *See* Athletics
Spring Hill Statement, 122
Stanford, Leland, Jr., 109
Stanford Linear Accelerator (SLAC), 44
Stanford Synchrotron Radiation Laboratory, 44
Stanford University: abbreviation custom at, 4, 51; founding of, 167; growth of, 9; institutional character of, 7–9; Kyoto campus,

113; "magic" of, 208–9; Washington, D.C. campus, 122
Stegner, Wally, 7
Stengel, Casey, 72
Sterling, J. E. Wallace, 71
Stevenson, Adlai, commencement quote of, 41, 55–56, 74, 84, 102, 119, 132, 160–61, 181, 203, 217
Strike, by United Stanford Workers, 42
Students: American Council of Education survey of, 101; as careerists, 18, 20, 105; relationship between faculty and, 6, 10–13

Tax reform, 85
Teachable moments, 200–201
Teachers: advice from, 2; improving quality of, 123–24; thanking, 39–40
Teaching, 211; at research universities, 106–11, 197–98; emphasized over research, 186–87, 188; evaluations of, 108; low status of, 68; preparation for, 172; quality of people entering, 20; science, 65–66, 123–24
Tenure, 86, 107–8
Tolerance: for ambiguity, 37–38; of diversity, 33–34
Training, education vs., 52–53, 71
Trustees: fiduciary responsibility of, 76–78; function of, 27; on president's speaking out, 24–25; trust and duties of, 77–78
Tuition, rise in, 88–91
Tutu, Desmond, 92
20–20 program, 192

Ujamaa, 135–36, 139, 140, 141
Undergraduate education: faculty-student relationship and, 10–11; quality of, 6; reflection on, 40; reformation of, 12–13; research

opportunities and, 11. *See also* Western Culture curriculum
Union activities: organizing clerical workers, 15, 25; United Stanford Workers strike, 42
Universities: finances of, 86–92; growth of, 8–9, 91–92; history of graduate schools at, 165–69; institutional character of, 6–9, 14; public positions on behalf of, 24–28; rankings of, 134–35; research, 106–11, 197–98
University of California at Berkeley, 9, 43, 170
University of Chicago, 167, 168
University of Oregon, human nature speech at, 45–49
U.S. News & World Report, college rankings of, 134–35
Utilitarianism: as institutional

character element, 7–8; need to go beyond, 22–23, 66–69

Values, 38
Varnedoe, Kirk, 209–10
Victoria yacht, 190, 191

Washington, D.C. campus, 122
Wasow, Tom, 134, 138
Western Culture curriculum, 3, 86, 103, 124–27, 129, 185–86
White, Andrew Dickson, 109
Wiley, Harvey, 117
Wilson, Woodrow, 166, 167, 171
Women's athletics, 30–33
Wright, Gordon, 107

Yeats, William Butler, 130, 131

Zare, Richard, 107